HOW to WIN at B2B EMAIL MARKETING

by Adam Q. Holden-Bache

Will —
Thank you for your support!
May all your campaigns be winners!
— Adam

Copyright 2015 by Adam Q. Holden-Bache
Published by Adam Q. Holden-Bache

Design and production by SPARK Publications
www.SPARKpublications.com

Charts and graphs by Jamie Allen

All rights reserved.

No part of this book may be reproduced, stored in a retrieval system, or transmitted by any means without the written permission of the publisher. The scanning, uploading, and distribution of this book via the Internet without the written permission of the publisher is prohibited. Your support of the author's rights is appreciated.

Printing History
Edition One, August 2015

ISBN: 978-1-943070-01-5

How to Win at B2B Email Marketing:
A Guide to Achieving Success

Dedication

This book is dedicated to all my fellow marketers.
May you all be winners in the end.

> The more difficult the victory, the greater the happiness in winning.
>
> - Pelé

> Boom, crush. Night, losers. Winning, duh.
>
> - Charlie Sheen

Contents

Part One:
B2B Email Strategy: Plan for Success 10

Why Email = Winning 11
- Email Marketing Is Essential to Business 13

Have a Goal 15
- Determining Your Goal 15
- Identifying Goals: Hard and Soft Metrics 16
- Success Indicators 17
- Using and Improving Benchmarks 17
- How to Get Results That Matter 17
  - Get to Know Your Data and Analytics 18
  - The Importance of Conversion Tracking 18
  - Develop Programs for Acquisition,
    Nurturing, Retention, and Re-activation 19

Who Is Your B2B Email Audience? 21
- Colleagues 21
- Marketing Agents 22
- Customers and Clients 23
- Business Buyers 23
  - The Financially Driven Buyer 23
  - The Solutions-Focused Buyer 24
- How B2B Is Different from B2C 24
  - The B2B Buyer vs. the B2C Buyer 25
- Where Do B2B and B2C Email Marketing Overlap? 27

B2B Email Marketing Trends and Challenges 29

Part Two:
Data: A Marketer's Gold Mine 34

Data Collection: Growing a High Quality List 35
- Permission-Based Marketing 35
- Data Collection 36
  - Optimize the Opt-In Process 36
    - The Opt-In Proposition 37
    - The Opt-In Form 37
    - After the Opt-In 39
  - Grow Your List: Where to Collect Data 39
  - Website Data Collection Options 42
  - **CASE STUDY:** FierceMarkets: Converting Web Visitors into Subscribers 44
    - Data Collection Fields 46
    - Progressive Profiling 47
    - Unsubscribe and Preference Centers 48
  - Use Caution When Renting an Email List 49
  - Why You Should Never Purchase an Email List 49

Using B2B Email for Lead Generation ... 53
Data Collection for Lead Generation ... 57
Winning Tactics after Data Collection ... 59
    Analyze and Revise ... 59
Alternative Ways to Generate New Leads ... 60

How to Manage Email Data ... 63
Data Hygiene ... 63
Data Integration ... 67
    Data Integration Goals ... 68

Deliverability and Authentication ... 69
Maintain Clean Data ... 70
Incorporate Email Authentication ... 71
    DKIM Authentication ... 71
    SPF Authentication ... 72
    DMARC Authentication ... 72
Engagement Matters ... 72

Part Three:
The Message: What You Need to Know ... 74

B2B Emails Don't Have to Be Boring ... 75
CASE STUDY: Indiemark: The World's Worst Email ... 75
Design Your Copy ... 77

Copywriting and Tonality ... 81
What's in It for Me? ... 81
Email Is Experienced in Stages ... 82
Stage One: The Inbox ... 82
    The From Name ... 83
    The Subject Line ... 84
    The Preheader ... 87
        Preheader Copywriting Strategies ... 89
Stage Two: The Email Body ... 89
Stage Three: The Landing Page or Website ... 93

Content: What Really Matters ... 97
B2B Content Idea Starters ... 99
Know Your Audience ... 100
CASE STUDY: Exact Software: Using Data to Generate Custom Content ... 101
Suggestions for Authentic B2B Communications ... 103

The B2B Newsletter ... 105
Newsletters Reach Decision Makers ... 108
What Not to Do with Your B2B Email Newsletter ... 108

Mobile: The New Standard ... 111
How to Create Mobile-Friendly Emails ... 113
    From Name ... 114
    Subject Lines ... 114
    Preheaders ... 114

TABLE OF CONTENTS

Content Considerations.. 114
    Design and Layout... 116
    Responsive Design.. 117

Beyond the Email.. 121
Winning Tactics for Landing Pages............................ 121
Winning Tactics for Surveys....................................... 122
Winning Tactics for Social Media............................... 125
Winning Tips for Video... 127

Part Four:
Know Your Audience: Deliver Relevance................ 130

Segmentation and Personalization.......................... 131
Personalization.. 131
    Email Personalization Options............................. 132
Segmentation.. 134
    Strategic Tactics for Segmentation..................... 134
    List Segmentation Strategies............................... 134
    Segmentation Options... 135
    CASE STUDY: UsedCardboardBoxes.com:
    B2B Email Alerts Lead to Big ROI........................ 138
Segment with Marketing Personas............................ 138

Lead Nurturing and the B2B Sales Cycle................. 141
What Is Lead Nurturing?.. 141
Why Use Lead Nurturing?... 141
What Role Does Email Play in Lead Nurturing?...... 142
Nurturing through the B2B Sales Cycle................... 142
Customizing Lead Nurturing Email Content........... 148
Lead Nurturing Challenges and Solutions.............. 149

Frequency and Cadence.. 151
Frequency With Targeting.. 153

Automated Campaigns... 155
Drip Campaigns.. 156
Nurture Campaigns.. 153
Content Stories for Automated Campaigns............ 157
Automated Campaign Frequency............................ 157
Marketing Automation Software............................... 158
    Tasks to Automate... 159
    Automation Headaches....................................... 160

Part Five:
Analysis: Review, Revise, Results............................ 162

Copywriting and Tonality.. 163
What Should You Test?... 163
Types of Testing.. 164
    A/B Testing.. 164
    Multivariate Testing.. 165
        How to Conduct a Multivariate Test............... 166

    CASE STUDY: Act-On Software: Responsive Design A/B
        Testing Leads to a 130% Increase in Clicks. 167
    Things to Test 170
        To Increase Revenue 170
        To Increase Click-Throughs 171
        To Increase Opens 172
        To Increase Revenue, Click-Throughs, or Opens 172
    After the Test. 173

Metrics: Analyze and Win 175
    Indicators and Results Drivers 175
        Analytics Data Sources 176
    Evolve Beyond the Open: Metrics You Need To Know 176
        Delivery Metrics 177
        Open Metrics 177
        Click Metrics 179
        Evaluation Metrics 179
        Website Effectiveness Metrics 180
        Micro-Conversions 181
        Financial Metrics 182

Determining ROI 185
    ROI = Return on Investment 185
    ROI Rules 186
    ROI's Role in B2B Marketing 186
    How To Generate Better ROI 187
    ROI Challenges and Solutions 188
    Reporting to Senior Management 188
    The Problems with ROI 189
        Marketing Value Versus ROI 189
        ROI Does Not Equal Profit 189
        ROI Doesn't Calculate Soft Benefits 190
        ROI Requires All Costs to Be Calculated 190
        ROI Misses the Big Picture 190

Part Six:
The Future of B2B Email Marketing 192

Emerging Concepts in B2B Email Marketing 193
    Dynamic/Agile/Real-Time Emails 193
    Fully Personalized Emails 194
    In-Email Transactions 196
    Cross-Channel Integration 196
    Putting Big Data to Use 197
    Micro-Segmentation 198
    HTML5 198
    Audio and Video in Email 199
    Visualization 199

ENDNOTES 202

ACKNOWLEDGEMENTS 210

How to Use This Book

This book is intended to be a guide to assist those who want to improve their business-to-business (B2B) email marketing results. *How to Win at B2B Email Marketing: A Guide to Achieving Success* will guide readers through all aspects of an email program, including strategy, data, design, copywriting, delivery, and analysis. Readers can step through the book sequentially or jump around from section to section depending on their current challenges or interests.

Throughout the book readers will notice icons highlighting important tips and takeaways. Pay special attention to these items as they will identify the content most likely to impact your marketing approach.

At the beginning of each chapter, the "Starting Line" will describe the email marketing challenges that chapter covers. Reading through these will help readers understand if their challenges are part of the chapter content.

At the end of each chapter, "The Winner's Circle" will recap the most important strategies and tactics from that chapter. This can be used as a review for anyone who reads through the chapter or as a summary of the key points of the chapter for those who need to digest the most important information.

The book's website (b2bemailmarketingbook.com) includes additional resources, case studies, and other information that will help keep readers informed of the most current happenings in B2B email marketing. Visit regularly, subscribe to the newsletter, and use the contact form if you'd like to reach out and connect with me directly. I'd enjoy hearing from you, and yes, I will personally respond.

PART ONE:
B2B Email Strategy: Plan for Success

CHAPTER 1
Why Email = Winning

Starting Line:

In this chapter you will learn:
- Why email is still a top communication channel
- Why email marketing is essential to business
- Why email is the most preferred channel for marketing messages

Email is considered "old-fashioned" by many. It isn't sexy. Many have labeled it "dead." (The *Wall Street Journal* did in 2011.)[1]

But it is the workhorse of the business world. There are 11,680 emails sent to the average worker each year.[2] On average, a worker spends 28% of company time reading and answering email.[3] It's no wonder that email continues to play a dominant role in business communications and marketing.

STAT **The average office worker checks their email inbox 30 times per hour.**[4]

Email is so ingrained in our business operations that we don't really stop to think about why we use it. What makes it such a successful platform? Why has it maintained its position as the top communications platform for so long? Why do marketers find it so valuable? The answers may be different to each user or business, but tucked in among these virtues are answers to all these questions:

1. Email is ubiquitous. Everyone has it, and because they do, it's a crucial tool. After all, what would you think of a business that didn't have email capabilities?

2. Everyone knows email. Email is a fairly simple tool. It's easily understood on both sides. Marketers understand that it's a great way to reach contacts. Recipients know that they have the power to manage their messages and act according to their best interests. It's a win-win for everyone involved.

PART ONE: B2B Email Strategy: Plan for Success

3. Everyone uses email. The use of email is not diminishing; in fact, it's growing. And it's growing a lot. Overall email volume is increasing 11.2% a year.[5] As long as email has been around, it's been a channel that has exhibited constant, steady growth. And its evolution continues.

4. People respond to email. Email response rates continue to confirm that people respond to email. It's the preferred channel for many consumers and businesses alike. An average worker spends 15% of each day reading email and 13% of a day responding to emails.[6]

5. It's sticky. People check their email. Frequently. Many people do it before they get out of bed in the morning. Many business professionals say it's the first thing they do to start their day. People rely on email, which is why they check it constantly. They act on email marketing messages. It's an important part of their professional and personal lives.

6. It's fast. Email marketing campaigns can be prepared quickly, especially when compared to other channels. Some marketers can turn around new campaigns in a matter of minutes. And delivery of those campaigns can happen in seconds. If a business has a need for speed, then its communication choice will almost always be email.

7. It's measurable. The beauty of email is that you can track results. In real time. You know how effective your marketing is within minutes of sending it out. From bounce backs to opens to clicks to conversions, all the data necessary for marketers to understand the effectiveness of their marketing can be analyzed instantly.

8. It can be targeted, segmented, and personalized. Need to reach a small portion of your list with an important message? Want to vary your messaging for each recipient? Want to create a unique message for each recipient? No problem. Email can do all that and more.

9. You own your email. Unlike other marketing channels like search and social, you own your email data and content. You are in control of your platform and messaging. You make your own email marketing choices and own every step of the process.

10. Email is cost effective. The cost of email marketing is so inexpensive that businesses tend to spend more on internal resources than on email platform or technology fees. There's no other marketing channel where you can provide as much value at such an inexpensive cost.

11. Email has a high return on investment. Due to its minimal production requirements and high conversion rate (especially when compared to other channels), email provides tremendous opportunity for businesses to realize a positive return on investment.[7]

96% believe the ROI of email marketing will remain consistent or will increase.

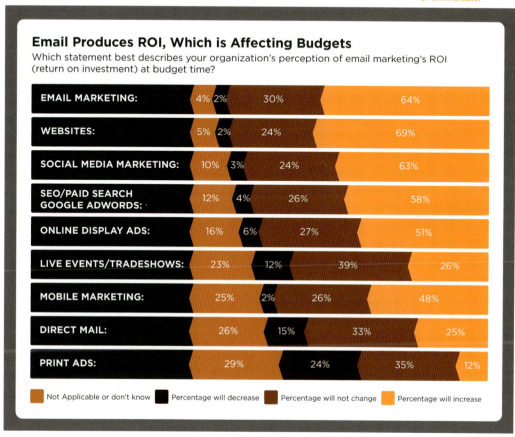

Email Marketing Is Essential to Business

Email marketing plays a very important role for the majority of businesses. A whopping 88% of marketers[8] believe that email marketing does or will produce a return on investment (ROI), and 68% of marketers say email marketing is core to their business strategy for a variety of reasons, the top being:

- Email indirectly impacts your business performance (42%).
- Email is a critical enabler of products/services your business provides (42%).
- Your business's primary revenue source is directly linked to email operations (16%).

Email is also the top-preferred channel for permission-based marketing messages. And it's not even close—77% of people

PART ONE: B2B Email Strategy: Plan for Success

prefer receiving promotional messages via email, while less than 10% prefer channels like direct mail, text messages, mobile apps, and social channels.[9]

Preferred Channel for Permission-Based Promotional Messages (by Age Group)
Promotional Messages From Companies Whom I Have Granted Permission to Send Me Ongoing Information

	OVERALL	15-17	18-24	25-34	34-44	45-54	55-64	65 PLUS
EMAIL:	77%	66	74	75	81	79	81	79
DIRECT MAIL (LETTERS, CATALOGS, POSTCARDS, ETC.):	9%	6	6	6	9	10	14	14
TEXT MESSAGING (SMS) ON A CELL PHONE:	5%	10	5	7	4	6	1	0
FACEBOOK:	4%	8	7	3	4	3	1	0
TELEPHONE:	2%	0	5	3	2	1	1	2
TWITTER:	1%	4	1	1	0	0	0	0
MOBILE APP:	1%	2	1	1	0	1	0	0
LINKEDIN:	0%	0	0	1	1	0	0	0

People are more than 7x more likely to want to receive promotional messages in their inbox versus any other channel.

Email provides the most direct line of communication to your audience, and it does so quickly and inexpensively. It drives awareness and interest, builds loyalty, and generates conversions. And to top it off, it is completely trackable.

Smart marketers know that email = winning.

Winner's Circle:
- Email is the workhorse communication channel. It's no longer sexy, but it delivers results.
- Everyone uses email. Everyone is comfortable with email. People respond to email. That makes it an ideal communication channel.
- Email generates a higher ROI (return on investment) than any other communication channel.
- Email is the top-preferred channel for permission-based marketing messages, and no other channel is even close.

CHAPTER 2
Have a Goal

Starting Line:

In this chapter you will learn:
- Why you need email marketing goals
- How to determine your goal
- How to establish and use benchmarks
- How to reach your goals

To win at B2B email marketing, you first have to understand the game. What are the right strategies? What defines success? How do you win?

It all starts with a goal. And everything you do should be focused on achieving that goal.

What is the goal of my email program?

This may be the most important question you can ask yourself as you prepare your B2B email messages. An email without a goal has negative effects for both the reader and the marketer. Recipients will not respond positively to any message where they have to figure out what to do. Marketers who send unfocused emails will see minimal activity, low response rates, and poor return on investment.

The goal should be obvious not only to you but to your recipient as well. If you review your email campaigns and the goals jump out at you, you're doing it right. If it's difficult for you to pick out the goal of your campaign, then it's back to the drawing board.

Determining Your Goal

The first and most important step in building a successful email program has nothing to do with email. Instead, it has everything to do with your business. You must understand your marketing objectives as your email program (and likely other non-email marketing activities) should be focused on achieving business goals.

TAKEAWAY

Without a goal you can't achieve success.

TIP

Always begin with the end in mind. Have a goal for your program.

PART ONE: B2B Email Strategy: Plan for Success

TAKEAWAY

Whatever will define success for your business is your goal.

Are you launching a new product? Rebranding your business? Entering a new market? Trying to generate leads?

Nothing will derail an email marketing campaign faster than a campaign that doesn't focus on the overall goals of your business (or one that focuses on too many goals simultaneously). A marketer must identify his or her business goal and begin preparing an email campaign with that goal in mind.

Identifying Goals: Hard and Soft Metrics

Goals can vary from business to business, but many campaign goals fall into either hard or soft metrics. Hard metrics are usually tied to financial success, while soft metrics are typically helpful for marketing insight.

Hard metric goals include:
- Increase revenue/sales
- Improve conversion rates (sales, opt-ins, downloads, sign-ups, etc.)
- Improve average purchase
- Generate more leads
- Generate better quality leads
- Reduce acquisition cost (per marketing sourced lead)
- Increase customer retention
- Shorten the sales cycle
- Lower internal costs

Soft metric goals include:
- Educate and inform (making a better subscriber or prospect)
- Improve sales/marketing alignment
- Improve insights on metrics and ROI
- Increase speed and agility for marketing campaign turnaround
- Improve internal resources (less time for campaign creation, management, and analysis)

For most marketers, email campaigns with soft metric goals will eventually lead to insights or result in improvements that will help campaigns with hard metric goals. For example, educating and informing a recipient could lead to a sale. The sale would increase revenue and improve conversion rates. In the end, hard metric goals move the needle and result in tangible business results. So if your campaign is focused on soft metric goals, determine how those can lead to improving hard metrics goals in the future.

Success Indicators

Once your goals are established, everything you do with your marketing should work toward achieving your goals. So how do you know if you're on the right track? There are many indicators of success. Indicators are not success metrics themselves, but they do provide insight into recipient engagement and the path taken to achieve success. Typical success indicators include:

- High deliverability rate
- High open rate
- High click-through rate
- Low bounceback rate
- Low number of spam complaints
- Low unsubscribe rate
- High number of forwards
- High number of social shares
- Increased website visits

Success indicators should not be used in place of campaign goals but may indicate why a campaign goal was improved or achieved. For example, if you change your call to action in your email and see a 20% rise in click-throughs, which leads to a 10% increase in conversions, then you can assume the rise in click-throughs was an indicator of your campaign's success.

Using and Improving Benchmarks

Once you understand your goals and success indicators, review your campaigns and see how they are performing. Are there any significant drop-offs in performance over your past campaigns? Any dramatic improvements? If so, try to understand why. Then analyze your results to determine an average for your success indicators. Set those as your baseline benchmarks.

The goal for your next campaign is to try to improve the performance of your baseline benchmarks by increasing hard metrics. For example, if your campaign typically averages a 25% open rate and a 2% conversion rate and then a change to your subject line bumps your numbers up to a 30% open rate and 3% conversion rate, you can assume your subject line change lead to an increased open rate that increased conversions.

How to Get Results That Matter

Winning email marketers know it's not just about getting results–it's about getting results that matter. Marketers need to have a way to define what results will help them achieve their business goals.

PART ONE: B2B Email Strategy: Plan for Success

TAKEAWAY

Constantly establish and refine benchmarks and try to improve them for every campaign.

In order to achieve those goals, marketers must set themselves up for success. To get results that matter, marketers must:
1. Implement tracking;
2. Make changes to a live campaign if necessary;
3. Track and measure success;
4. Identify points of failure and change them; and
5. Understand how results can be analyzed to determine ROI.

Get to Know Your Data and Analytics

There's only one place to understand the difference between success and failure, and that's in the data. Successful marketers spend hours reviewing data and analytics reports. They slice, dice, and dig into the results so that they have a full grasp on what worked, what didn't work, and where there's room for improvement.

B2B email marketers should get to know the analytics reporting tools and functions they have available to them. They not only need to know their email platform tracking features, but also how to access data and get results from other marketing platforms such as their website analytics, CRM tools, databases, automation software, call centers, customer support, e-commerce platforms, sales teams, and more.

Knowing how to access this data PRIOR to pushing the "send" button is imperative. Marketers should set up pre-campaign trials in order to test everything they need to track and analyze campaign results. It's always a good idea to run a full test to ensure all tracking so that a full analysis of the campaign can be completed after it is delivered.

The Importance of Conversion Tracking

If you can't determine whether or not a recipient completed an intended action, you can't evaluate the success of your campaign. Since conversion tracking is the holy grail of marketing analytics, it must be planned and set up prior to any campaign activity.

For some B2B email marketers, this means setting up landing pages or using trackable links or working with their IT or web team to embed tracking pixels in websites so that any post-email activity can be determined. It may also mean understanding what data can be captured or accessed, and how that data can be used to help you understand marketing activity.

In many cases a conversion from a marketing campaign may take place beyond the digital realm. A marketing email could initiate a phone call, a direct connection with a marketing representative, filling out and submitting paperwork, or some other action. If the goal of your campaign is to initiate that conversion, it is important to find a way to track that conversion activity prior to your campaign delivery. This may mean working with your inbound call center to make sure they include a question like "how did you hear about us?" when taking orders; it could require adding a field to your CRM application to track the source of a lead; it could also mean adding something that can be input (coupon code) or scanned (QR Code, bar code, etc.) from a printed document at the point of sale.

And no matter how well you prepare and how diligent you are with your tracking, there will always be scenarios where you won't be able to track every conversion. Someone somewhere will click through on that year old email at the bottom of their inbox. This holy grail of metrics is never truly attainable, but it is important to try to track and analyze as much of the conversion process as possible.

Develop Programs for Acquisition, Nurturing, Retention, and Re-activation

The first programs many B2B marketers initiate are aimed at retention; they often use newsletters for this purpose, and many businesses stop there. The goal of newsletters is to keep recipients informed of business activity, new products, services, and case studies that will educate and provide insight on the sender's business. But businesses that are truly committed to using email for customer retention will also send emails to existing customers to show their appreciation of their relationship through personalized content, educational materials, product or service announcements, and more.

When businesses focus on programs built around acquisition and nurturing, they are aiming to move contacts through the sales cycle. Acquisition and nurturing programs are meant to educate and provide incentive to recipients so that they migrate from a soft lead to a purchase. These programs can be extensive and may require many messages. Each message may be scheduled and delivered based on a period of time, a user action (such as an open or a click), or an event trigger. Many businesses rely on marketing automation software for these programs to assist in managing the rules and activity from these campaigns. *(We'll explore automated campaigns further in Chapter 18.)*

PART ONE: B2B Email Strategy: Plan for Success

Brands that try to re-engage non-active subscribers will find value in awakening value out of dormant contacts. Many businesses find that large parts of their database go "dormant" over time. Recipients won't open emails, but they won't unsubscribe either. Identifying and targeting these contacts with special offers, information, or other custom messaging can help re-engage the contact and return them to an active subscriber. Re-activation programs can be highly beneficial to almost all businesses but can particularly benefit those with older contacts or those with low open rates.

Winner's Circle:
- You can't achieve success if you can't define success. As a first step, identify the business goals for your email campaigns.
- Identify success indicators, so you can see which parts of your campaign are working well and which need improvement.
- Determine benchmarks, and try to improve your benchmarks for every future campaign.
- Understand how to get results that matter. Do the work required before campaign delivery, so you can track and measure results.
- Make sure you can track conversions that occur online via email or website and offline via phone call, point of sale, or other personal interaction.

CHAPTER 3
Who Is Your B2B Email Audience?

Starting Line:

In this chapter you will learn:
- What types of audiences make up a B2B marketer's database
- How you should focus your marketing approach based on the different audiences
- Who are different types of B2B buyers
- What the differences are between B2B and B2C (business-to-consumer) purchasing behavior
- How B2B buyers require a different marketing approach than B2C buyers
- What similarities exist between B2B and B2C email marketing

B2B email marketers tend to have a wide variety of contacts in their email databases. When you understand the different audiences and speak to them appropriately, your email marketing will be much more successful. Moreover, when you segment these audiences and provide relevant, valuable content, you'll find it much easier to establish trust, gain credibility, and move your audience toward a conversion.

Marketers need to understand their business relationships with their various contacts in order to collect and manage data properly, segment accordingly, and prepare meaningful messages.

Let's take a look at these various types of audiences that likely make up the majority of a B2B marketer's existing contact database.

Colleagues

Many larger businesses may find themselves marketing to recipients within their own organizations. Email may be the chosen communication platform to inform colleagues of a product launch, new services, changes in business operations, or other important news.

B2B marketers will need to prepare messaging that speaks specifically to this audience. Since they are potentially part of that audience

PART ONE: B2B Email Strategy: Plan for Success

themselves, preparing effective communications shouldn't be a hard concept to grasp. Put yourself in the role of the recipient, and you can analyze the effectiveness of the email.

Because the email is coming from the brand they work for or a senior level member of the organization, the open rates will likely be high for the communication. Recipients will pay attention to these messages and will process the information as it is pertinent to their jobs. If the email has directives or calls to action, they should be clear and concise to avoid any potential misunderstandings.

In email marketing campaigns where co-workers are the intended audience, corporate brand and legal compliance, design, copywriting, and tonality may be of higher importance here as every internal best practice will need to be perfected in order to meet corporate expectations. Spend the time and effort necessary to ensure the communication does the job it was intended to do, and make sure that nothing included has any negative effect on any person or part of the organization.

Marketing Agents

Many B2B companies will have marketing agents—local representatives that will be the contact for the sales of corporate products and services. These agents come in many varieties: brokers, resellers, sales representatives, franchisees, distributors, etc.

Because these agents ultimately represent the success or failure of your marketing efforts, they can be the most important contacts in your database. These agents may also represent other brands, so it's critical to make your communications stand out from the competition and encourage the marketing agents to want to do business with your brand.

TIP

When communicating with marketing agents, beware of sounding "salesy."

Remember that marketing agents are not buyers. Many communications will be intended to inform and educate so that the agents can succeed in their marketing efforts. With a proper understanding of the value and benefits of a particular product or service, marketing agents will be more likely to promote that item with their sales contacts.

When marketing to these agents, you are setting an example of how your brand should be represented. The design, tonality, copy, and content needs to be high quality so that agents take a similar high-quality approach when they represent your brand.

Customers and Clients

Even companies that are primarily B2B marketers will occasionally find it necessary to contact individual customers or clients. Sometimes a direct connection will be in place of a communication from a marketing agent, and sometimes it will be on behalf of a marketing agent. These types of communications tend to include news or updates about a product or service; they might include corporate news and information important to existing customers or clients.

Message tonality should be warm and friendly but also professional and polished. Marketers must strive to keep these relationships strong so that the customers and clients will want to continue their business with their brand and hopefully grow the relationship and increase retention.

 65% of B2B buyers concur emails shape their view of a company's brand[10]

TIP
Because you already have a business relationship with these contacts, it is important to acknowledge that relationship and do whatever possible to strengthen those ties and increase the value of your brand with those individuals.

Business Buyers

Increasingly, business buyers are researching purchasing decisions online long before they engage with sales. This empowers them with information, of course, but during this research they will also be influenced by many non-marketing factors including existing professional relationships, peers, budgets, existing infrastructure, resource availability, and much more.

The business buying cycle can be long and arduous. Winning over modern business buyers requires organizations to revolutionize their marketing approach, and the barriers to success are vast. This is why winning B2B marketers speak to buyers' price concerns and business requirements.

Businesses need to understand what motivates buyers. Are their purchasing decisions more influenced by price or solutions? Typically buyers will consider both, but in the end, one of the two will play the larger role in influencing the final decision.

The Financially Driven Buyer

The financially driven buyer is making a decision based on price, but other factors may influence their perception of what the overall price will entail. These factors include support options, maintenance costs, upgrades, internal expertise, and training.

Questions you may need to anticipate from a financially driven buyer include:
- How many months of support are included with the initial purchase?
- What hidden costs will I incur by implementing your solution, such as power consumption or bandwidth?
- How often will upgrades occur, and how will they be implemented?
- If we need additional training, how much will that cost?

The Solutions-Focused Buyer

The solutions-focused buyer is making a decision on how well a new product or service will solve existing business problems. These buyers may be easier to identify as they will likely research information about how a new solution will compare to an existing setup, and they might ask questions via email and social channels.

Providing educational materials, case studies, and other informative content will likely help you identify these buyers and lead them to an appropriate solution.

Questions you may need to anticipate from a solutions-focused buyer include:
- Will your product or service solve my existing issues?
- Is your product compatible with my current business setup?
- How much training is involved in order to be up and running?
- How do you provide assistance or support?

Buyers will want to choose a partner that can solve existing business challenges and better prepare for future challenges. A solution that offers power when it's needed but doesn't result in complexity will have an advantage over its competition.

Smart buyers will plan for growth and will evaluate options based not only on existing features but also for flexibility and a history of product or service improvements. They understand that a business or service with a history of growth, innovation, and new feature implementation will likely continue to evolve as it matures.

How B2B Is Different from B2C

We all make B2C purchasing decisions on a daily basis. We make these decisions almost instantly based on our purchasing goals. Do we purchase the loaf of bread because we like the brand or because it's on sale? Do we go to the gas station based on convenience or due to lower prices? Do we eat at a restaurant because it's closest to home, because it offers healthy foods, or because we know the owner?

Many consumer purchase decisions are made quickly, and many times they are emotionally triggered. Favorite jeans on sale for 30% off? OK, let's get them. Having a bad day? Grab that candy bar in the checkout line.

But in B2B marketing, there are very few times when decisions are quick and emotional. B2B purchasing decisions involve much more consideration. The business environment, constraints, and buying process all influence the final purchasing decision.

The B2B Buyer vs. the B2C Buyer

A B2C buyer is typically focused on buying a product or service for the cheapest price from a brand they trust. B2C marketing is about earning that trust and then making offers that connect with the B2C buyer in order to create a sale. If B2C marketers earn enough trust and provide enticing deals, the buyer won't bother to research price or features. They'll have an emotional connection and follow through with the purchase without putting in time to research or compare prices.

A B2B buyer is likely to be quite different. They are usually knowledgeable about a product or service, they will spend time researching and comparing, and they know they have to make an informed decision so that it benefits their business. And they most likely won't be making a decision quickly nor will they do it alone. Both buyers will consider other factors when making a decision. Customer support is relevant to both B2B and B2C buyers. Customer support helps build customer loyalty as buyers know they can count on a company to make sure they have positive purchasing experiences. Poor customer support can create such a negative effect on buying that even the most amazing offer or the most intriguing deal won't generate a sale.

B2B marketing is different from B2C in at least 10 ways:

1. Longer sales cycle. B2B sales cycles can typically be several weeks to several months and in some cases even a year or more. B2B email marketers need to recognize the longer sales cycle and prepare proper marketing tactics for each part of the cycle.

2. Relationship driven. Building relationships is key in B2B sales, and the longer sales cycle, when handled properly, gives the B2B marketer plenty of opportunity to build strong ties to eventual buyers. Sometimes these relationships will rise above all other factors during the decision-making process.

3. Niche target market. One of the nice things about B2B marketing is that marketers typically have a smaller, more defined target audience. The bad news is that there are a limited number of prospects. Make every communication count.

4. Education required. In a B2B sales cycle, businesses tend to interface directly with potential customers multiple times in order to inform and educate the prospect. Email marketing can play a big role in this process. Businesses can use email to provide a continuous stream of educational content that can ultimately influence the final purchasing decision.

TIP

In your emails, provide content that the recipients can use to influence group decisions. Provide information sheets, presentations, or other collateral that they can print or share with their colleagues. Make it easy to have your marketing materials reviewed by groups of people.

5. Complexity. Meeting your goals in a B2C relationship could be achieved with one communication. Retailers do this all the time through sales and promotions. B2B relationship are much more complex. B2B marketers must provide relevant information about their products and services, educate, nurture, and be available for response. Post purchase, they must continue the relationship and assist with implementation, training, support, and anything else required to strengthen the relationship. And all this must be done at the right time to the right audience.

6. Information Driven. B2B marketers make a majority of their purchasing decisions based on the information they are provided or based on information that they research. Providing relevant information to B2B marketers via email can help lead recipients toward a purchasing decision.

7. Group purchasing decision. For many business-focused email campaigns, the goal is not to get an immediate reaction but to get the email read and to get its information presented to the right person within the recipient's organization. Sometimes the marketing contact is not even the lead in the decision-making process but rather a data-gatherer.

8. Considered decision-making process. You have to approach B2B buyers as experts since 85% of them conduct Internet research at some point during the buying process. The research typically involves product or service data gathering, competitive analysis, and reviews of third-party feedback (comments, testimonials, etc.). All this, along with your marketing messages, will factor into a very well-researched decision-making process.

B2B email marketers should acknowledge this and provide links to as much relevant web-based information as possible.

9. Enterprise level purchases. A B2B purchasing decision can be a significant investment–not just financially, but also through the future commitment of time and resources. Buying decisions will be based on how a product increases productivity, increases revenue, decreases risk, or decreases resource time and/or expense. To secure a B2B purchase, the price is usually not the only factor. Quality of support, product history, integration compatibility, and many other factors need to be considered.

10. Turnover. With the instability of the business marketplace and increasingly higher employee turnover, B2B contact databases are becoming more and more susceptible to losing contacts faster than they are gaining them. It's not uncommon for 20 to 30% of a marketing database to become invalid over the course of a year. B2B marketers will need to understand their turnover rates and do their best to retain customers who are changing addresses but remaining prospects. Preference centers and other data capture forms can help B2B marketers keep as many contacts as possible. Experienced B2B marketers know that business decisions are rarely impulsive, while consumer purchases are often so. Keep your messaging focused on a positive long-term experience.

Where Do B2B and B2C Email Marketing Overlap?

As we've seen so far, B2B and B2C marketing typically have different approaches. But due to email marketing and the technical limitations of it as a marketing channel, there are some additional areas of B2B and B2C overlap.

1. Interactions in the email channel are brief. You typically only have seconds to make an impact. A recipient will review your message and quickly decide whether to delete it, read it, or save it for later. You have to provide enough value to make your message stand out in a crowded inbox.

2. Relevance, targeting, and timing contribute to success. Whether you're a B2B or B2C marketer, you have to provide a relevant message to the right audience at the right time to reach your desired outcome. Sending bad content to those who don't want

TIP

Help your audience do their research and lead them to your most favorable content.

TIP

Use email as a way to promote all the benefits of your product or service so that buyers are well informed and comfortable with everything you have to offer.

TAKEAWAY

Experienced B2B marketers know that business decisions are rarely impulsive, while consumer purchases are often so. Keep your messaging focused on a positive long-term experience.

PART ONE: B2B Email Strategy: Plan for Success

to receive it not only diminishes the results of your campaign but also creates a negative brand experience that can hurt your email marketing efforts and the overall value of your brand.

3. Learn from your results. You should learn something about your recipient with every email you send. That may be positive (clicked on a link) or negative (didn't open the email). B2B and B2C marketers know that reviewing your campaign metrics, analyzing results, and using that data to make changes will improve future marketing performance.

4. It's all about the relationship. People buy from brands they like and trust. And that's based on relationships. In a good relationship, a buyer may overlook price or features in order to do business with a brand or person that they like.

TAKEAWAY

Relationships trump nearly everything in business. Successful brands have successful relationships.

Winner's Circle:
- Your marketing will be much more successful when you understand your different audiences and provide appropriate messaging to each.
- Messaging should be optimized to speak to the differences between colleagues, marketing agents, customers and clients, and business buyers.
- When marketing to business buyers, try to understand if solutions or price will ultimately determine their purchasing decisions.
- B2B purchases are much more considered than B2C purchases. They are less influenced by emotion and are more influenced by research, business environment, and business goals.
- There are many ways B2B marketing is different than B2C marketing. Recognize these differences, and prepare your marketing messaging accordingly.
- Segment your B2B messages for your various audiences, and keep your B2B messaging focused on your long-term goals.
- Both B2B and B2C purchases can be influenced by relationships. Relationships trump price and features. Successful brands have successful relationships.

How To Win At B2B Email Marketing

CHAPTER 4
B2B Email Marketing Trends and Challenges

Starting Line:

In this chapter you will learn:
- Why email is the most important B2B marketing activity
- What email marketing goals are common in the B2B industry
- What email marketing challenges are common in the B2B industry and how to identify areas for improvement

B2B marketers are email marketers. Nine in ten (88%) B2B businesses take advantage of email marketing. And nearly one half (44%) deliver email marketing messages at least once a week.[11]

When asked about the most important B2B marketing activity, email leads the way. It beats out social media, blogging, search, webinars, white papers, mobile, and all other channels by a wide margin.[12]

Nearly two-thirds of respondents rank email as a top digital marketing priority.[13]

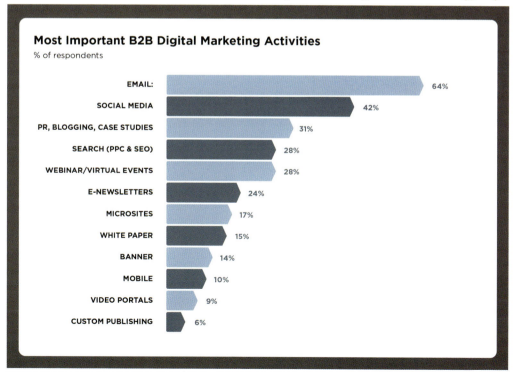

Most Important B2B Digital Marketing Activities
% of respondents

Activity	%
EMAIL:	64%
SOCIAL MEDIA	42%
PR, BLOGGING, CASE STUDIES	31%
SEARCH (PPC & SEO)	28%
WEBINAR/VIRTUAL EVENTS	28%
E-NEWSLETTERS	24%
MICROSITES	17%
WHITE PAPER	15%
BANNER	14%
MOBILE	10%
VIDEO PORTALS	9%
CUSTOM PUBLISHING	6%

29

PART ONE: B2B Email Strategy: Plan for Success

Email is likely considered the most important B2B marketing activity due to its ability to generate revenue. Between 2013 and 2014, revenue from email has increased by 28%. Companies are attributing 23% of their total sales to email marketing, compared to 18% in 2013.[14]

When marketers were asked how they rate various marketing channels in terms of return on investment, email marketing ranked as the top channel with 68% of companies rating it as "good" or "excellent."[15]

Email marketing rated the top marketing channel for ROI.[16]

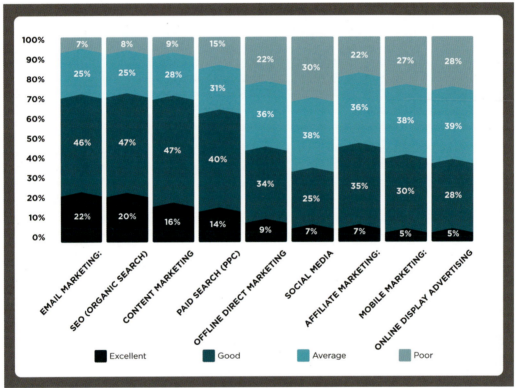

Email campaign success rates vary widely based on the message content, the offer, and the quality of list (as well as hundreds of other factors). And although marketers should be focused on the success of their campaigns, many like to know where they stand against industry averages. If that holds any value to your organization, the B2B industry averages are:[17]
• Open rate: 11 to 18.7%[18]
• Click-through rate: 2.1 to 5%

And if you want to compare the email marketing industry averages (including B2B and B2C):
• Open rate: 31%
• Click-through rate: 4.4%[19]

30

When it comes to the email marketing goals, B2B marketers are pursuing the following objectives:[20]
- Generating and nurturing leads: 78%
- Enhancing/building brand: 68%
- Driving sales: 59%
- Strengthening thought leadership: 52%

Even though lead generation and nurturing is a primary goal of most B2B marketers, only 30% are using email as their primary lead generation tactic.[21] Many marketers have found email to be more effective for nurturing the lead after acquisition than using it to obtain leads.

Despite the popularity and success of email, a whopping **65% of B2B businesses are allocating under 25% of their marketing budget to the channel.**[22] Perhaps this speaks to email being a lower cost channel as compared to others, but in many situations, email marketing budgets do not equate to the success that the channel delivers.

For those who are not satisfied with the results of their campaigns, B2B marketers have cited the following areas as options for increasing effectiveness:[23]
- Subject matter: 55%
- Subject line: 40%
- Database relevance: 39%
- Database accuracy: 38%
- Personalization: 32%

Relevant offers are crucial to successful campaigns. B2B email marketers have found some of the most effective offers are invitations to a webinar, followed by white papers and case studies. Content types such as freebies, discounted services, and limited-time offers are not as popular.

In order to improve B2B email marketing effectiveness, marketers need to test. Testing provides key insights into what works and doesn't work within a campaign. It's a mandatory practice for any marketer who wants to improve the results of their marketing efforts.

The most common testing techniques for B2B email marketers include:[24]
- Types of content: 58%
- Correlation between subject line and open rates: 57%
- Time of day: 46%

TAKEAWAY

If your numbers are lower than industry average and your campaign is profitable, then there's no need to change your approach. If your numbers are better than industry average but you aren't turning a profit, then your campaigns are not as effective as they should be.

PART ONE: B2B Email Strategy: Plan for Success

No matter what you send or what you test, email is only valuable if it achieves positive results for your business. So whenever you review industry statistics, trends, or tactics, always use the information to find ways to improve your results. What matters most is that your campaign is meeting business goals and objectives. But never settle, and always try to refine and improve.

Winner's Circle:

- Email marketing is the most important B2B marketing activity according to 64% of B2B marketers.
- When it comes to generating ROI, email has been rated as a "good" or "excellent" marketing channel by 68% of marketers.
- Email marketing industry averages are somewhat useful for comparison, but the only thing that really matters is if your campaigns generate positive business results.
- Even with the success of email marketing, the majority of B2B marketers allocate less than 25% of their budget to the channel.

PART TWO:

Data: A Marketer's Gold Mine

CHAPTER 5
Data Collection: Growing a High Quality List

STARTING LINE

In this chapter you will learn:
- Why you should only collect permission-based data and the value of doing so
- How to optimize the opt-in process
- What to consider when preparing a data collection form
- How to grow your email list
- Where the most effective places are to capture data on your website
- How to craft a well-architected unsubscribe process
- Why you should not rent or purchase an email list

Your email marketing efforts are only as good as your list. The size and quality of your subscriber list is a direct indicator of how successful you will be at reaching your email marketing goals.

For many businesses, email list growth is difficult to achieve. In fact, only 17% of businesses report a rapidly growing list.[25] Half say their lists are growing, albeit slowly. The good news is that very few businesses report shrinking lists. But what this does prove is that it's harder than ever to create list growth, and many are not experiencing the growth they desire.

Permission-Based Marketing

Permission-based marketing is defined as obtaining permission from a recipient before adding them to your marketing process. For email marketers, this consent is typically earned when someone fills out a web form to submit their data, thereby creating an "opt-in."

Permission-based marketing does not include using data that is found or purchased and used without the consent of the recipient. This may include purchasing a list of email address data or by harvesting email addresses off a website or other source.

TAKEAWAY

Increasing email list size and list quality should be a top priority for B2B marketers. By doing so, marketers will have a greater chance of increasing leads, improving business relationships, increasing sales, and improving their ROI.

PART TWO: Data: A Marketer's Gold Mine

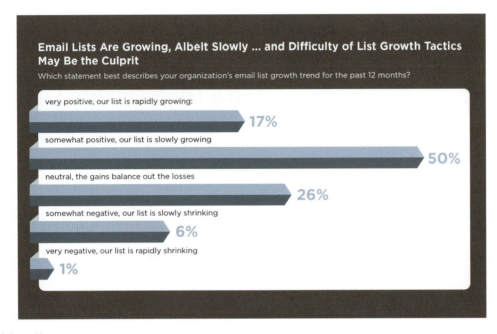

Half of all email lists experience slow growth.[26]

Using non-permission-based data for email marketing will typically backfire on today's marketers, as it will likely result in deliverability issues. If you send to a large database of invalid email addresses or if too many recipients mark your email as spam, your campaign could be flagged and not reach other valid email addresses at the same domain or addresses under the control of that ISP (Internet Service Provider).

Data Collection

The better your data collection process, the better your list's growth rate and quality. Why? The means by which you collect subscribers is one of the first marketing experiences you will have with many of your new list members. Creating a positive experience for them from the beginning will reap rewards further into the marketing cycle. A primary goal of building an email list should be creating a rewarding experience for your subscribers.

Optimize the Opt-In Process

Unfortunately, one of the most overlooked parts of most email marketing programs is in the opt-in process. To get the most out of your email lists, you'll want to personalize and target the best recipients by gathering relevant subscriber data. This starts with preparing your opt-in pages and forms so that they will affect both your list's growth and quality.

> **TAKEAWAY**
> Your best bet is to try and attract the audience you desire, provide value in exchange for their personal information, and maintain a database free of invalid or expired user records.

> **TAKEAWAY**
> Always be sure to offer value in exchange for subscriber marketing data.

36

The Opt-In Proposition

Subscribers will provide their contact data to brands, but only under certain circumstances. Subscribers need to know that they'll have a positive business experience in exchange for their data. To entice subscribers, marketers must communicate the following to subscribers during the opt-in process.

1. Value. Subscribers want to know that they'll receive valuable information, insights, education, promotions, or deals if they sign up for your email list. Make sure to let them know what kind of content they'll receive when they subscribe, or better yet, share an example of an email they'd receive.

2. Frequency. Disclose how often you plan to send them messages and what type of messaging they can expect to receive. Do not send them content outside of what they've requested.

3. Control. Subscribers want to be in control of the relationship. Make sure they understand that they can unsubscribe at any time or control their preferences for frequency and content.

4. Privacy. Make subscribers feel secure that their data will be protected, and including a link to your privacy policy is never a bad idea.

The Opt-In Form

The form itself requires a lot of consideration. You need to capture the data required to segment, personalize, and optimize your campaign. However, you don't want to risk turning away potential opt-ins with a lengthy form. Over the past few years, website opt-in forms have been asking for less information up front. In fact, one-third of opt-in forms only require an email address, and 14% of all forms are asking for less information when compared to opt-in forms five years ago. Marketers who collect less data at opt-in should round out a contact's data profile by incrementally asking for additional data (through surveys, event sign-ups, download forms, etc.) or by matching it with existing data.

What you choose to collect will be based on your business needs. In order to get the best results from your opt-in form, consider these best practices:

1. Make it easy. If you want to get email opt-ins, make your opt-in form visible. Don't bury it in the footer of your home page or make it an email icon stuck next to your social media icons. A marketer with a high opt-in rate will place it in a prominent position on their home page and

PART TWO: Data: A Marketer's Gold Mine

have it visible on other pages throughout the site. And it should be mobile friendly too, so any visitors from mobile devices can easily find the opt-in form and input their personal information.

2. Ask for only the information you need. At minimum, you have to collect an email address and maybe a first and last name. If you plan on using other data to segment your lists, such as location, ask for that as well. **Do not ask for data that you do not plan on using.** The more you ask for, the more wary the subscriber becomes. At a later time you can follow up with an email asking for more information, or you can ask subscribers for more information when you have a good use for it. You can also acquire additional data through a subscription center, survey, data appending, or other forms.

One-third of all opt-in forms only request an email address.[27]

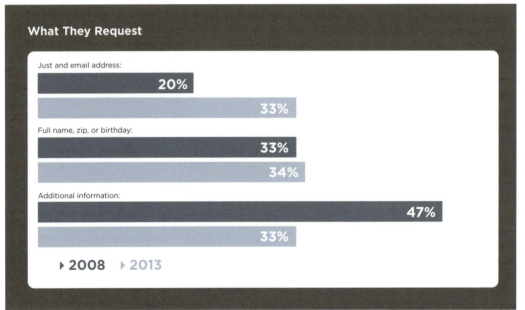

What They Request

Just and email address:
- 20%
- 33%

Full name, zip, or birthday:
- 33%
- 34%

Additional information:
- 47%
- 33%

▸ 2008 ▸ 2013

3. Do not pre-check opt-in boxes. You can trick people into signing up for additional email subscriptions, but do you really want to email subscribers who didn't ask to receive your content? This has the potential to annoy recipients and increase your spam complaint rates and can have legal repercussions (it's actually illegal in Canada due to the Canada Anti-Spam Law). Let the user select what they want to receive.

4. Validate your data. During the opt-in process you may want to include a captcha to prevent bots from entering bad data. A captcha will ensure that you have a human submitting their information. You may also want to validate the data in real time to prevent bad entries. For a very minimal cost, services such as BriteVerify and LeadSpend will make sure that email addresses being submitted are valid before they go into your database. This will ensure that your captured data is clean, which will prevent deliverability issues. Sending emails to bad addresses not only adds additional marketing expense, but too much of it may result in your valid addresses seeing your emails go to their spam or bulk folders.

5. Send a welcome/confirmation message. After sign-up, immediately send a confirmation email (or begin an on-boarding series of emails). Thank them for subscribing and re-iterate how their data will be used. Present them with a special offer. Make them feel secure that they are dealing with a legitimate marketer and that being part of your list will be beneficial to them.

After the Opt-In

Once you have the data you need, you must use it, and you must use it wisely. Marketers who have collected enough data that would allow for segmentation or personalization but choose not to use it are demonstrating marketing laziness.

1. **Deliver on what you promise**. Once you have opt-in subscribers, respect their privacy and continue to deliver relevant, interesting, usable content.

2. **Timing is everything**. Make sure you have the resources and budget to communicate to your opt-in database on a consistent basis. Make sure there's not a dramatic time gap between the opt-in and the first communication.

3. **Respect your database.** Make sure your opt-in subscribers understand they are valuable to you. Respect their privacy and treat them as you would want to be treated.

Grow Your List: Where to Collect Data

You may be surprised to learn that most marketers do not collect the majority of their new email records on their website. In fact, 58% of marketers estimate that they acquire one-quarter or less of their email subscribers on their corporate website. Only 21% say three-quarters or more are collected there. So if marketers are not collecting email addresses through their websites, where are the addresses coming from?

Today's multi-channel marketing environment provides more options than you might think. And they aren't only for B2C marketers. Here's a list of 21 places beyond the standard opt-in form where B2B marketers could collect email marketing data.

PART TWO: Data: A Marketer's Gold Mine

1. Surveys. Create a survey and provide an incentive for completing it. Ask for user data to send the reward, and then provide an opt-in to receive other offers or content via email. Promote the survey everywhere: on your site, in social channels, via your blog, etc.

2. Offline events (conferences, seminars, trade shows, meet-ups). Whenever you're at an event, collect data from those you meet. If you are not running a booth or table, ask people you meet if they'd like to opt-in to receive your email content. If they agree, have them sign up on-site either using a mobile website data capture form on a mobile app that allows for data collection (many email service providers provide mobile apps that work online or offline). If that's not possible, follow up with them via email after the conference, providing a link to your opt-in form. Always allow the person to sign-up themselves, rather than doing it for them, as you'll see a considerably lower unsubscribe rate.

3. Registration for downloads (white paper, e-book, etc.). Provide a newsletter opt-in checkbox when people are providing their data to access your downloadable content.

4. Online events (webinar, virtual conference, etc.). Ask for email opt-in when users sign up for your webinar or virtual conference.

5. Point of sale. Ask for the user's email address during checkout. Many consumer-focused marketers have been doing this for years, and it's also an effective tactic for B2B marketers. To ensure better data have the user enter it themselves on a touchpad or terminal, and provide an offer or benefit to them immediately after sign-up.

6. Inbound sales and support calls. Instruct your sales and support teams to collect email addresses when people call in to either team.

7. Facebook page. Promote and provide incentive for your Facebook page visitors to opt-in to your email list. Give visitors a reason to sign up.

8. Twitter. Ask your Twitter contacts to opt-in to your email newsletter. Offer a reason to join. The day before you send your email, announce what it'll include to pique people's interest.

9. LinkedIn and LinkedIn groups. LinkedIn is a great place to generate interest in your email content. And you can do it in multiple ways. Provide incentive for your employees to ask for sign-ups via their status updates. On your corporate page, provide a link and an incentive. Within LinkedIn Groups, provide relevant content first (be helpful), and then provide a link if you think your connections may want to stay in touch with the services and information your business provides via email.

10. Videos. If you create video content, showcase your email opt-in URL at the end of your video and in the video description if allowed.

11. Social channel promotions. If you have any kind of event or content download, promote those offers in your social channels in order to get people to the content and opt-in form.

12. Sweepstakes/promotions. Sweepstakes are certainly one of the fastest ways to collect new addresses, but the quality of leads can be somewhat suspect. Regardless, even B2B companies can create a highly targeted sweepstakes or promotion that generates substantial interest and dramatically increases leads.

13. Email signatures. Use all email correspondence to promote your email content. Ask for a sign-up in the signature area of your emails.

14. Print materials. Adding a URL to printed marketing materials is common practice, but also consider other print materials where you can encourage recipients to sign up. Brochures, receipts, and trade show collateral can all include a URL or QR Code to get readers to the opt-in form on your website.

15. Direct Mail. If you send direct mail, ask for the opt-in to allow those interested to stay in touch. Provide incentives such as special offers, email-only content, or educational material.

16. QR codes. Use QR codes to your advantage in your print publications, collateral, in store, advertisements, etc. Provide a QR code with a link to your email opt-in form. Since you're working with a mobile audience when using QR codes, make sure your opt-in form page is mobile friendly, and don't ask for more than the email address unless absolutely necessary. Collect additional profile data later.

17. Mobile apps. Add an email opt-in to your mobile app. Include it in the account settings, during an intro, or within the app itself.

18. Mobile text subscription. If you have a large audience at a conference, seminar, or other event, consider a mobile subscription option to gather new opt-ins. "Text CODE123 and your email address to 55555 to sign up for X." It's unique, and with such an easy opt-in process, it may invoke enough curiosity to generate a significant number of leads.

19. Your blog. If your blog attracts many new visitors, make sure you integrate your blog and email marketing. If you keep it at the top of your sidebar, make sure it stands out. Also consider adding a pop-up

PART TWO: Data: A Marketer's Gold Mine

for first-time visitors, and perhaps add a form at the end of each post or in the footer.

20. Your website. When it comes to collecting opt-ins on your website, you'll want to consider the basic placements (such as the home page) and the less obvious placements as well. Explore your entire website and look for opt-in opportunities that aren't just on the home page or in a sign-up or download form. And make sure you have an opt-in feature for any registration components, such as event sign-ups and content downloads.

21. Sponsorships and Promotions. Ask for email addresses in exchange for anything you provide of value. Giving out something for free? Ask for an email in return. Highspot took advantage of this when it was the sponsor for free WiFi at a marketing conference. This landing page with email data capture appeared after the user accepted the terms and conditions. Note the additional incentive of a free sales playbook.

Capture email addresses in exchange for valuable content.

Website Data Collection Options

The most popular ways of capturing email addresses on websites are on a dedicated email page (58%), on the home page (56%), in the footer (38%), in the header (15%), or in a pop-up window (2%).

Many marketers who use pop-ups or popovers and header/footer placements notice a rise in their subscription rates. A pop-up opt-in is a web form that appears in a new browser window or tab. A popover appears as a form that lays over the current webpage. A popover is also sometimes referred to as a lightbox. Here is an example pop-over signup form from eMarketer:

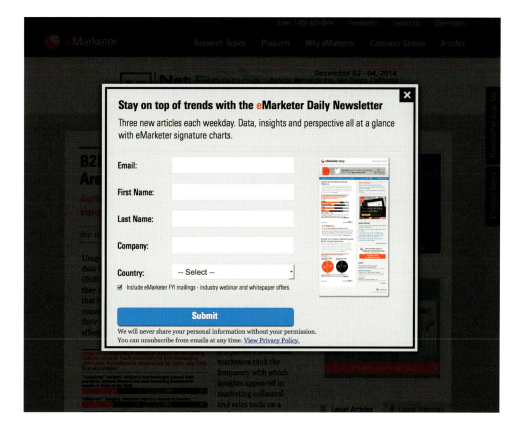

Many businesses that have implemented popover subscription options have noticed a significant increase in opt-ins. Various brands have claimed growth of 200 to 400% with some even saying they've seen a ten-fold or more increase.

Marketers should consider whether or not a popover is right for their brand. A popover is interruptive and will keep visitors from experiencing the content they've come to your site to access. But many understand the reason for the popover and will not hold it against a brand. They'll simply close it and move on if they aren't interested. And if marketers implement a popover to only appear upon new visits or have it go away after several displays, it likely won't interfere with a visitor's activity on your website.

Most brands may want to test implementing a popup or popover to see if it increases subscriptions. There's a lot of upside and little danger if implemented correctly. Make sure you measure your subscription rates and home page or landing page activity before implementation, so you can use it to benchmark against your analytics after the popup or popover is active.

PART TWO: Data: A Marketer's Gold Mine

CASE STUDY

FierceMarkets: Converting Web Visitors into Subscribers

FierceMarkets, a digital B2B publishing company, generates up to 80% of its email newsletter list growth from visitors to the websites of its 48 publications. They have taken an aggressive approach to attempt to convert visitors into subscribers, and it has paid off.

FierceMarkets makes it easy for visitors to subscribe to its email newsletter list by offering no less than four signup areas on each of its content pages. The pages include a yellow "pusher" area at the top (it pushes content down as it expands), a signup box in the right column, a one-line signup link in the middle of the content article and a signup form at the bottom of the page.

On top of these opt-in options, FierceMarkets also places an interstitial that appears after a web visitor's first click. The interstitial includes the four most important data fields. It will disappear with a click on a

How To Win At B2B Email Marketing

"No Thanks" link or clicking anywhere outside the form. It also appears only once every 24 hours to minimize invasiveness.

After entering an email address in any of the email address boxes, a visitor is taken to a second page requesting additional demographic data. Even if the visitor doesn't provide any additional data on the second page, they are still subscribed. But FierceMarkets has found that 72% of people do fill out the additional demographic fields, which provide a rounded customer profile.

As for effectiveness, it seems that the more invasive the position of the signup, the better it converts. The "pusher" and the interstitial placements have the highest conversion rate.

PART TWO: Data: A Marketer's Gold Mine

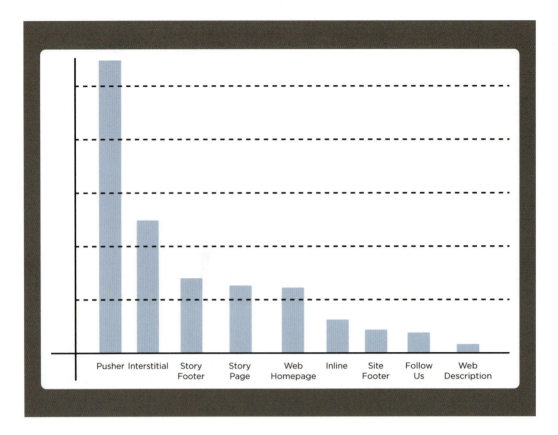

Like with so many other tactics in email marketing, it's important to gather data and review results to determine what works best. For FierceMarkets, they've learned how to maximize their web visitor-to-subscriber conversion rate through the testing of multiple invasive, non-invasive, and traditional opt-in form placements.

Data Collection Fields

Choosing what data to collect during opt-in can be a challenge for many marketers. Do you make it quick and easy and only ask for an email address, or do you include several more fields to get a better contact profile and risk losing some potential opt-ins?

Start by determining what data you must have in order to start an effective email marketing process. For some marketers this is only an email address. For others, data for segmentation may be necessary. If a particular product or service is only available in certain regions, collecting a zip code may be mandatory. If knowing a job role is necessary in order to partner the contact with the correct marketing persona, collecting a job title may be a mandatory field.

How To Win At B2B Email Marketing

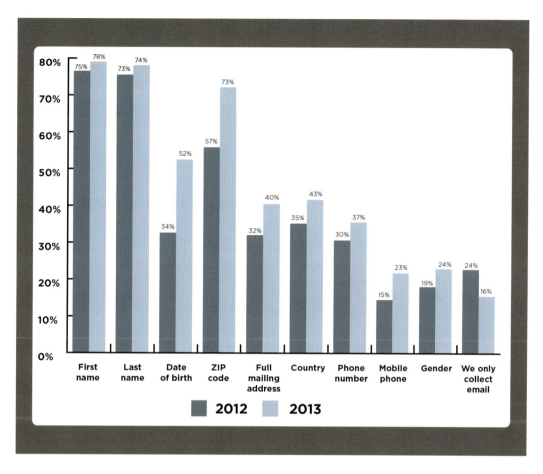

Along with many other parts of your marketing, opt-in forms should go through a testing process to determine what generates the best response rates and/or the highest quality opt-ins. Consider testing:
- Number of data fields
- Mandatory/optional fields
- An offer or promotion
- Call-to-action language ("Download Now," "Free," etc.)
- Headline copy
- Imagery
- Links and/or button styles

In addition to an email address, marketers frequently collect first and last name, zip code and date of birth data.[28]

Progressive Profiling

Whatever data you collect initially, you can continue to add more data layers to each subscriber record over time. Consider using a multi-step opt-in form to have new subscribers round out their profiles. You can also collect data in a variety of ways from tracking clicks on links in emails to appending subscriber profiles from data collected when signing up for a webinar or downloading a whitepaper. As you build a more complete profile for each subscriber, use that data for segmenting or personalizing email message content.

47

PART TWO: Data: A Marketer's Gold Mine

Unsubscribe and Preference Centers

Managing unsubscribes is a sometimes overlooked part of the data management process. A well-constructed unsubscribe process with an ability to manage communication preferences may allow marketers to maintain relationships that would otherwise be terminated.

Over the past few years many marketers have found that allowing recipients to manage their communications (receive fewer emails or receive emails only with specific types of content) may keep recipients from unsubscribing. This is common practice for a quarter of all marketers and is one of the fastest-growing techniques to maintain existing email relationships.

Unsubscribe best practices continue to improve, and nearly all marketers stop sending within 10 days of unsubscribe requests. [29]

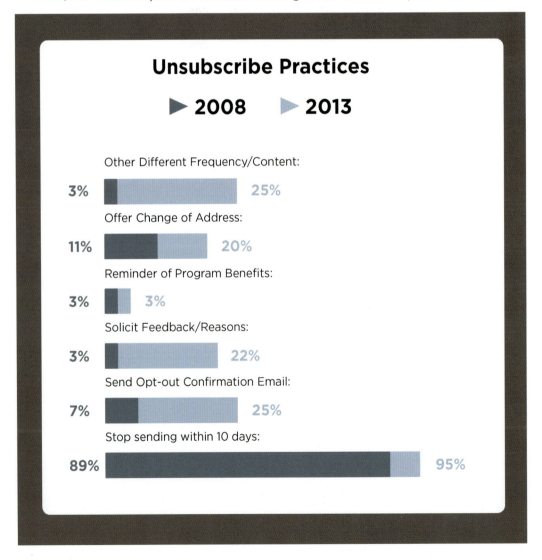

Many marketers are also now soliciting feedback from unsubscribes so that they may better understand why recipients are removing themselves from the marketing process. This kind of data will shed light on areas of improvement and give marketers ways to improve their email marketing efforts. Marketers may also try to move those unhappy with an email subscription to their social channels, so they may maintain a relationship and engage them in an alternate channel.[29]

Use Caution When Renting an Email List

Renting an email list has the potential for both positive and negative consequences. A legitimate list rental opportunity can help you gain exposure to a new audience. Renting a list of marginal quality can result in little to no activity and a negative brand experience.

When a marketer rents an email list, they provide a marketing message that is delivered by a list owner to their subscribers. The marketer never sees or acquires this list. They pay a fee for this service, usually on a cost-per-thousand basis (prices can range from $1 to $500+ per thousand contacts).

For the best results, marketers should only rent a "single-source subscriber list," which means the list data comes only from one source such as a publication, association, media channel, or non-competitive product/service. Many marketers find value in associating their brand with one of these other brands in order to derive value through brand association.

Marketers should avoid renting a list that uses data acquired from multiple sources or from any sources that cannot be identified. The email list seller should be able to produce data acquisition sources upon request.

Marketing value will come from the responsiveness of the list rental subscribers, so marketers will need to provide a valuable offer that makes sense to the subscribers of the rented list. If executed well, marketers can leverage the brand association to generate exposure, grow their lists, and generate revenue.

Why You Should Never Purchase an Email List

Email marketing is all about relationships. Relationships are built on relevance and trust. When you purchase an email list, you're sending to contacts with whom you have no relationship. It's very likely your email is not something they want. It's not something they've asked for. You're being disruptive. Is that how you want to begin a professional relationship?

Purchasing an email list is often one of the worst tactics an email marketer can employ. There are few instances (if any) where a purchased list has generated positive return on investment. Marketers are usually better off putting their budgets into content, search or referral marketing, website improvements, or some other marketing approach that will make them more visible and findable to those who are looking for their products or services. And that in return will help you build a quality in-house list.

Here's why you don't want to purchase an email list:

1. You're putting your reputation at risk. Purchased lists may consist of bad addresses or honeypot email records (an email address that has been set up specifically to identify spammers) that will result in a high number of bounces or will be identified by ISPs as spam. Those bad records can get you blacklisted, and that could be a big issue, especially if you are sending from the same platform as your legitimate campaigns. While B2B-specific email lists may have fewer of these issues, it's still important to understand that you can never be sure of the quality of the addresses you purchase.

2. You'll be labeled as a spammer. Recipients who don't recognize your from name may click the "spam" button in their email software. You'll be identified as a spammer by the recipient and the ISP.

3. Understand that reputation affects deliverability. Spam filtering was once determined by monitoring content. However, this approach necessitated lots of rules and analysis to determine which messages were legitimate and which were spam. Additionally, spammers quickly learned how to work around this by frequently adjusting their content. The modern approach to email deliverability is largely based on several attributes such as the sender's IP address and domain, whether or not authentication is in place, historical data, and more. Your sending reputation will be a factor in deliverability not just short term but long term too. If you choose to send to purchased lists, know that you could be setting yourself up for a range of deliverability issues well into the future. Is that a risk you're willing to take?

4. You could have legal issues. In the United States, it is a legal requirement under the CAN-SPAM Act of 2003 (enacted in 2004) that any email solicitation must be labeled as a solicitation and reference who you are and what you are soliciting. In all unsolicited emails, the CAN-SPAM Act requires senders to include their physical address and business contact information. Senders may not hide, alter, or use fake aliases or give misleading information in their from name, from email or subject line. And they must include an opt-out (unsubscribe) function. If you do not adhere to these laws, you could put your business in a risky position that could lead to legal issues. And if you send email to Canada, the CASL (Canada Anti-Spam Legislation) will also require your compliance.

5. It's not effective. According to the 46% of B2B marketers that use third-party email lists, only 11% score the tactic at "four" or "five" on a five-point scale of effectiveness (with "five" being the most effective), and 57% score the tactic at "one" or "two."[30] However, when sending to an in-house list, these numbers are almost a complete reversal. Of the 95% of B2B email marketers who send to an in-house list, 67% consider the tactic a "four" or "five" in terms of effectiveness, while only 5% consider it a "one" or "two."

6. The reward is not worth the risk. Why spend your marketing budget to damage your brand and be labeled a spammer? There are so many better ways to achieve your marketing goals. List buying is simply not a wise choice.

High quality emails are expected and anticipated by recipients. That's why a quality database is a marketer's gold mine. It's the source from which all marketing revenue flows.

Purchased lists are the exact opposite. They're a source from which negative relationships flow. When you interrupt someone with your email campaign, you'll do damage to your brand and your reputation and could potentially hurt deliverability for future legitimate campaigns. Don't risk making a first bad impression. You'll only have one chance, so do it right.

PART TWO: Data: A Marketer's Gold Mine

Winner's Circle:
- The size and quality of your subscriber list is a direct indicator of how successful you will be at reaching your email marketing goals.
- By increasing email list size and list quality, B2B marketers will have a greater chance of increasing leads, improving business relationships, increasing sales, and improving their ROI.
- Only collect data through permission-based marketing processes.
- Be sure to offer value in exchange for subscriber marketing data.
- When collecting data, only ask for the fields you require. Do not ask for data that you do not plan on using.
- Grow a quality list by asking for and collecting data in multiple channels.
- Allow recipients to manage their email preferences, and ask them to change them instead of unsubscribing. You may maintain a relationship that is otherwise lost.
- Never rent or purchase an email list. It's not worth the damage you can do to your brand, both present and future.

CHAPTER 6
Using B2B Email for Lead Generation

STARTING LINE

In this chapter you will learn:
- How B2B email marketing can drive customer acquisition
- What the steps are for a B2B email lead generation campaign
- How to optimize your data collection process
- What to do after you've collected data
- What alternative paid options are available to generate leads

B2B email marketing is widely considered a great channel for customer nurturing, sales, and retention, but it seldom gets its due as a customer acquisition tactic. Many marketers undervalue email as a way to introduce their brands and initiate relationships, with the goal of creating quality leads that can eventually be converted into sales.

Acquisition is often considered one of the most difficult challenges facing B2B marketers. Generating high-quality leads is something that over three-quarters of all marketers rank as their most difficult challenge—even more so than generating a high volume of leads and marketing to a lengthening sales cycle.[31]

But email can be used for acquisition if executed properly. Email marketing can be extremely effective for lead generation. In fact, 42% of B2B marketers cite email as being their most effective lead generation channel when targeting new customers.[32]

STAT **73% of marketers say email is effective at generating leads, and 58% say it directly leads to sales[33].**

The steps for B2B lead generation email campaigns include:

1. Create A valuable offer. The key ingredient to lead generation is offering something relevant with a high perceived value that's useful to your target audience—something that solves a problem. For many of us, that offer will come in the form of content. The most

PART TWO: Data: A Marketer's Gold Mine

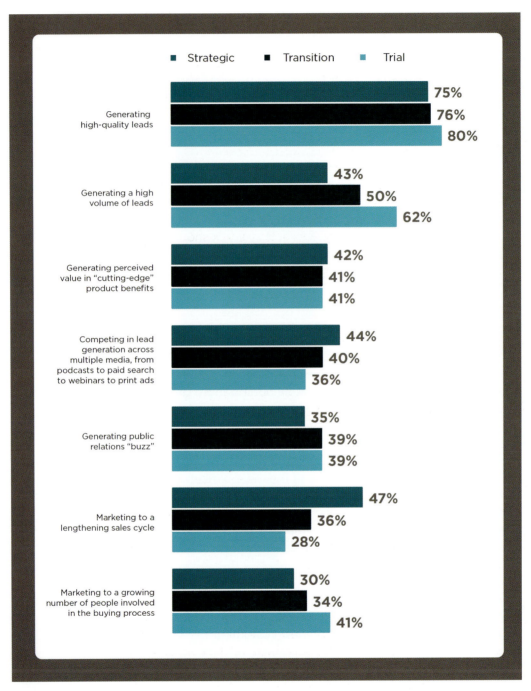

Generating high-quality leads is the biggest challenge for B2B marketers.[34]

popular content marketing formats include white papers, e-books, and webinars.

Because the offer is key to your lead generation success, make sure you produce something that users will want, will share, and will be eager to provide personal information in order to access it.

2. Create the email. Everything in the email should focus on benefits to the recipient. The email needs to get the recipient to understand how accessing the offer will help them save time, save money, save resources, or become more educated about a particular topic.

The email should have a strong call to action, and it should create urgency. It's also advised that marketers create several emails with various subject lines, calls to action, and call-to-action placements. Test each with a small sample, and deliver the winner to the majority of your recipients.

3. Build a landing page. The email is just the first step in the lead generation process. You'll need a landing page where the recipient will go to get more information, fill out a form, and then ultimately access or download the content. The landing page needs to be clear and easy to understand. It should be a quick experience and get users directly to what they want—the content. The landing page should include the same offer as your email and should have a similar look and feel.

The experience from the email to landing page should be seamless. Users should have no doubt that they're taking the next step toward accessing the content they desire. The landing page will be your opportunity to capture the lead by requiring users to fill out a form to access the content.

In this example from Movable Ink, the email clearly promotes an e-book and provides a clear call-to-action. When the user visits the landing page, they can easily provide their personal information to gain access to download the e-book. Moveable Ink not only requests their data for e-book download, but also adds an email signup form to capture opt-in data for those that may not want to provide all their personal data to gain e-book download access.

PART TWO: Data: A Marketer's Gold Mine

Movable Ink

The Mobile Takeover Survival Guide

Tips and Tricks for Email Marketing Success in the Mobile Inbox

With 66 percent of all brand marketing emails now being opened on smartphones and tablets, mobile is now the predominant vehicle for consumer engagement with email communications. Yet so many marketers still seem to be in a "desktop first" mentality, or find themselves struggling with optimizing campaigns for the mobile inbox.

In this eBook, we will share how the email marketing landscape has rapidly shifted from a desktop-dominated one to a mobile-dominated one, and offer examples and best practices for surviving in the age of the mobile takeover.

Get the eBook

Ready to be inspired? Get the e-book today.

Copyright © 2014, Movable Ink. All rights reserved.
636 Avenue of the Americas, 5th Floor
New York, NY 10011

Not interested? Unsubscribe

Movable Ink
636 Avenue of the Americas
5th Floor
New York, NY 10011

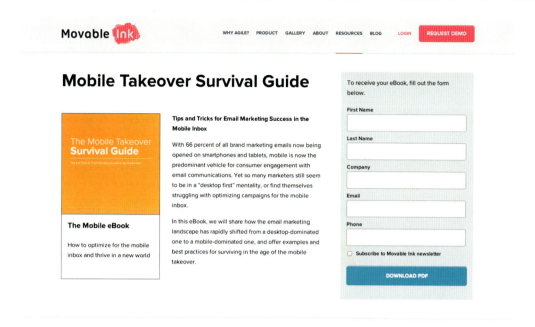

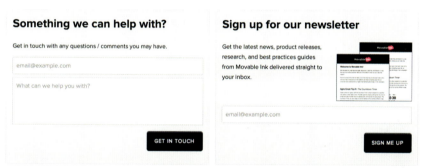

Data Collection for Lead Generation

As an email marketer, your list is everything. Marketers are challenged with continuously growing their lists, so it is imperative that the data collection process is optimized to be as effective as possible.

To maximize the effectiveness of your opt-in process, consider (and test) the following:

1. Explain benefits. When a visitor arrives at your registration form page, many will be leery of completing the form without knowing

PART TWO: Data: A Marketer's Gold Mine

what they'll get in return. If you clearly demonstrate the benefits of completing the registration form, then your chances of acquiring lead generation data improve dramatically.

This is why, when building your registration form, you should make sure the benefits are announced prior to the form area, and maybe even show an example of what they'll receive. Make them want to complete your form, so they can take advantage of what you have to offer.

2. Give thought to your registration form length (hint: keep them short). Roughly three-quarters of marketers don't collect any data from subscribers other than an email address. But when collecting additional data, the most popular pieces of data collected by marketers are first (75%) and last (73%) name, ZIP code (57%), country (35%), date of birth (34%), and full mailing address (32%). Interestingly, while 30% collect a phone number, only half that proportion collects a mobile phone number.[35]

It's been proven that visitors are leery of providing too much personal information up front without knowing the benefits of what they'll receive in return. People also want a quick and efficient experience. So only require the basic information you need to establish communication and build a basic customer profile.

3. Decide which fields are mandatory. About three in ten marketers said they don't make any field other than the email address mandatory.

TAKEAWAY

If you collect the data, make sure you use it.

Email marketers are adopting more tactics to track behaviors and acquire subscribers' preferences and interests in order to market to them more effectively. So consider which fields are absolutely necessary for your marketing segmentation purposes and which are ones you can add or append later.

4. Use standard form-field names. Many browsers have an auto-complete feature that will automatically fill in the names of common fields, such as first name, last name, and email. If you want to expedite the opt-in process, using these standard field names will allow visitors in certain browsers to have their data auto-populated, which will dramatically cut down on the time it takes to complete the form.

5. Make opt-in permission clear. If you are collecting data at various sources and want to add registrants to your newsletter list, make sure the checkbox or whatever other indicator you are using clearly states that they will be added to that marketing list. Make the user confirm

58

their interest by having them check the box. Don't pre-check it assuming they'll want to be added. You'll collect less data, but what you have will be completely permission-based, and that will help with deliverability and reduce your spam complaints.

6. Confirm legally required data. Most B2B marketers won't have an issue with attracting under-age visitors, but if you think you may run that risk, make sure you're compliant with COPPA (Children's Online Privacy Protection Act). And if you do business internationally, make sure you have permission to mail to countries in the European Union.

Winning Tactics after Data Collection

Once you've collected data, send an auto responder confirmation and thank you email with a unique offer and added value content (such as your latest blog posts, case studies, white papers, etc.). Also provide links to other relevant content, like a corporate blog, as well as links to your social channels.

Keep in mind that this is now the beginning of a customer relationship—hopefully a long one. You want to establish trust and become recognized as an authority in your field. If you promise more than you deliver with your initial offer, you'll get the relationship off on the wrong foot. But if you over-deliver, you'll have a much more positive effect. Recipients will be more receptive to your next communication and will likely be more willing to become an active prospect.

Once the relationship is established, you can use your email communications to nurture the relationship, convert the recipient to a customer, and then continue using email for customer retention.

Analyze and Revise

Once the campaign is delivered, your job is not complete. You'll want to review the performance of your campaigns, see what worked and what didn't work, and adjust as necessary to improve future communications.

Your new prospects will also require attention. You'll need to make sure that your data processes are set up so that any opt-in records will flow into the lead nurturing process and that they'll start receiving emails that will educate them and move them toward purchase. You want to be top-of-mind when they're ready to buy.

PART TWO: Data: A Marketer's Gold Mine

Alternative Ways to Generate New Leads

Generating new leads can be a huge challenge for B2B marketers. Most marketers rely on the data collection tactics discussed in the previous chapter. But what if you need to find new leads quickly and have a budget to get your message in front of a new audience?

Here are some paid lead generation options that you may want to test with your business.

1. Single-source email list rental. Many B2B publishers and organizations will send an email message (typically a "sponsored" message) to their own databases of recipients for a price. The marketer will produce the email message and supply it to the sender. The sender will deliver the email to its list of recipients as a piece of sponsored content. Senders will provide the marketers with results. Marketers can assess their success rate by analyzing traffic from the email to the landing page, website, call center, or other destination.

Costs of email list rentals will vary based on list quality, audience, and volume.

Example: BtoB Online (previous to acquisition by AdAge)
Audience: 40,000 Opt-in Email Subscribers
Cost: $275/CPM

2. Content publishing on third party sites. Some B2B publishers will allow you to place content in their libraries or resource centers. By adding your content to their site you'll position your company as a knowledgeable resource and increase your exposure to the audience that the site attracts.

When you provide content such as white papers, research, or webinars, the site publisher will provide the complete contact information of any visitor that downloads your content. Many sites will also assist in advertising your content through sponsored emails, ad units, text ads, and other forms of advertising.

Example: BtoB Online White Paper Library (prior to AdAge acquisition)

Cost: $3,000 for 50 leads ($60 cost per lead) or $6,000 for 109 leads ($55 cost per lead)

3. Sponsored or co-branded content. Many publishers offer custom editorial content that marketers can brand or sponsor. Editorial may include reports, research, white papers, or other content. Some content is developed directly with the marketer in mind, and the marketer may influence the topic and collaborate on research or content development. Other times the content may be already developed, and the marketer can select content based on what they think will help them attract interest.

The final product is a piece of content that can be downloaded or accessed from your site or the publisher's site, or can be printed and used how the marketer best sees fit. If you choose to make it accessible via download, it can be a sure-fire way to attract a targeted audience.

Examples:
AdAge BtoB Editorial Sponsored Research
Cost: $10,000
AdAge BtoB Co-Branded Sponsored Research
Cost: $17,000 ($20,000 with whitepaper; $35,000 with webinar)

4. Co-sponsored content. Being one of several sponsors on a piece of content may be a hard idea to stomach, but by doing so you can dramatically cut your cost per lead. This option works out well if you have a solid lead nurturing program as you'll need to stand apart from the other sponsors after you secure the lead. In most cases the other sponsors will be non-competitive, but you'll still want to make sure your product or service is the one that receives the most attention and is first in line for a sale.

Keep in mind that many B2B buyers research many brands and products and will sign up for anything that they feel they need to research or review prior to making a decision. B2B purchases are considered, and nearly every purchase is made after a deliberate review of all options. So your competitors will be in the mix, and your job is to rise above them. Don't think that your brand will be the only one a buyer contacts prior to making a purchase. If you have that mindset, you'll realize co-sponsorship may afford you a better cost per lead and increase your ROI.

Costs will vary based on content and number of co-sponsors.

5. Buying a data file or email list. Although buying lists is NOT recommended, if you have no other option but to purchase one, then you should choose the right vendor. Choose a vendor that offers high-quality B2B data that can be segmented based on industry, job title, job function, owner, years in business, etc.

If you must purchase a list, talk with the vendor about list quality, where the data was sourced, how often it is verified, and guaranteed deliverability rate. If anything feels sketchy about the data you are purchasing, it probably is. In most cases you pay for what you get, so select wisely.

Winner's Circle

- A great offer, email campaign, and landing page can be a primary source for generating leads, which is usually described as the most difficult challenge facing B2B marketers.
- Optimize the effectiveness of your opt-in process by explaining opt-in benefits, only collecting the data you require, and using standard form-field names.
- After collecting data, immediately send a thank you or confirmation email with a unique offer and links to relevant content.
- Constantly analyze campaign performance and adjust to improve future communications.
- Make sure your opt-in process flows into your lead nurturing process so that you move your recipients toward purchase.
- Consider other email acquisition tactics like email list rental, content publishing, and sponsored content if you need access to data quickly or if you have enough budget to test these tactics.

CHAPTER 7
How to Manage Email Data

Starting Line

In this chapter you will learn:
- How to cleanse your email marketing data
- How to validate email marketing records
- How to allow users to manage their own data
- How to integrate email marketing data with other platforms

A successful email marketing program requires quality data. B2B email marketers know that managing data is one of the most challenging parts of running a successful email program. The number of channels where data resides has grown and continues to do so. Data is now gathered from email, CRM, social, mobile, websites, micro sites, surveys, events, and more. Because this data typically exists in silos within its own channel, organizing and utilizing this data can be a huge challenge for many organizations.

So how do B2B marketers manage data and use this wealth of data to their advantage?

The challenge is to harness the data you need to help you reach your business goals. Start with the basics, proceed from there, and automate as much of the process as you possibly can.

Data Hygiene

Most marketers probably have in-house data but may be unsure of the quality of that data. In order to determine if the data will be effective, marketers can use a variety of tactics to ensure it is usable and make sure it will not introduce any data or deliverability issues.

1. Cleanse your data. If not already performed during data collection, one of the first steps marketers should do is run a syntax check to correct any email address formatting issues. Run the data to make sure all records use properly formatted email addresses and to eliminate typos. Some issues you can easily check include:

- Email addresses include an @ sign
- Email addresses include an extension
- Email addresses do not include spaces
- Email addresses do not include non-ASCII characters

Also look for mistakes made during data entry or typing issues. Search for data problems and continuously make a list of items to fix. Here's a short list of things to check:

- Domains that end with additional punctuation such as ".com." or ".net.". Search for the additional period after the extension as people will accidentally do this during data entry.
- Data that ends in multiple extensions. Look for records with ".com.com" or ".net.net". This happens on occasion during data entry when fields are short and visitors can't see the end of their address when they enter it.
- Emails that have the extension omitted (personname@companyname without a ".com" or ".net").
- Misspellings of domain names such as "yhoo.com", "gmial.com" or "outloook.com".
- Multiple "@" signs such as "person@companyname@com".
- Double periods such as "person@companyname..com".
- Honeypot or non-personal email addresses (also called "role account" email addresses). Search your database for email records such as "sales@", "webmaster@" or "info@" and remove those from your database.

2. Validate email data. Once your data has been cleansed of formatting issues, you'll want to check its validity. This means making sure the data is current so that your email contacts will receive your email communications.

Marketers can check for Domain Name Systems (DNS) resolution to ensure domains exist and that MX records exist for the domains. An MX record is a type of resource record in the DNS that specifies a mail server responsible for accepting email messages on behalf of a recipient's domain.

Marketers can also use an email verification service such as BriteVerify or Leadspend to make sure all the email records in their lists are still deliverable. These services will flag dead domains and invalid email addresses, so you can update or remove those records from your database. By doing so, you'll decrease the risk of lowering your sender reputation and increase the likelihood that your emails reach recipients' inboxes.

How To Win At B2B Email Marketing

If you notice a large amount of bounces from a business domain, you may want to make sure that the business is still operating and confirm that the company name hasn't changed. If it has changed its name, you may be able to update those records with the new domain information and keep those contacts in your database.

3. Allow users to manage their own data. A preference center is a destination where users can go to manage their personal data and their email subscription information. Users should be able to update their names, email addresses, other personal details, and the email lists to which they subscribe. Along with that, they may also be able to update their email preferences such as frequency and types of messaging.

Providing a preference center has many advantages. It will allow users to update their personal information, which may keep them subscribed even if they change jobs or email addresses. It will also allow them to manage what they want to receive. So if you send frequently, allowing them to say how often they want to receive may be the difference between keeping a relationship or having them end it.

Below is the Dell Subscription Center where recipients can manage their subscriptions and preferences. The "Subscriptions" tab allows recipients to manage their business segments and the types of messages they want to receive, and the "Preferences" tab allows them to select product interests.

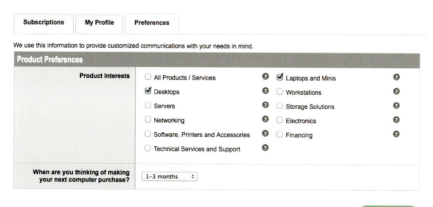

PART TWO: Data: A Marketer's Gold Mine

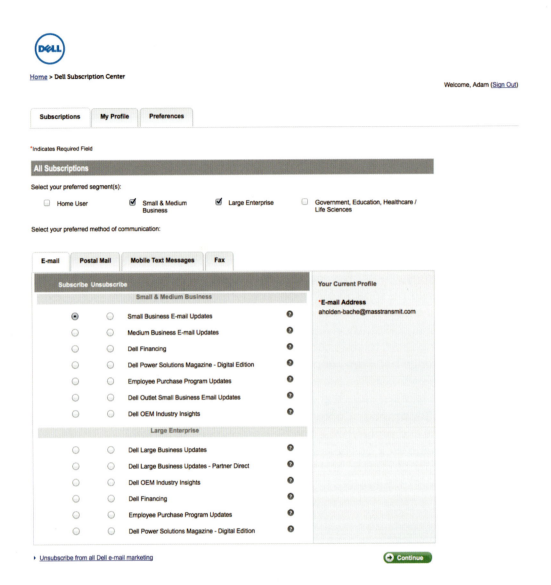

Here's how Grainger handles its preference center. Its highly visual interface is very intuitive. It's easy to view and edit your personal information and email preferences, and it's clear how to fully unsubscribe.

How To Win At B2B Email Marketing

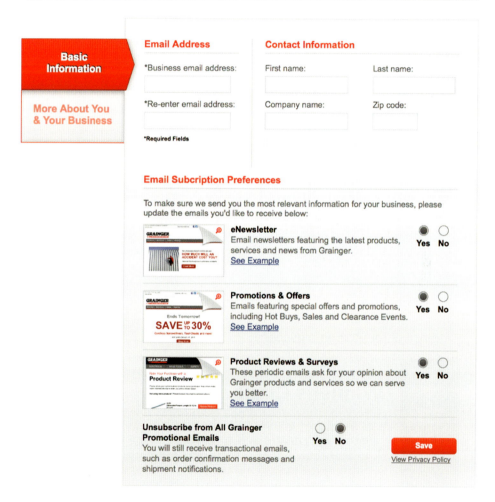

Data Integration

Many businesses rely on software to help them manage their prospects and leads. Your sales team may already be using a database, a CRM (customer relationship management) platform, or an integrated marketing platform to track the progress of those connections.

PART TWO: Data: A Marketer's Gold Mine

The problem many businesses experience is that email is responsible for a large part of the progress made with those connections. And email is not always easily integrated with their data processes or CRM platform.

Over the past few years many platforms have improved their capabilities or merged with other platforms to seamlessly integrate CRM and email. But many businesses still have legacy systems or established data processes that make dealing with email and CRM data difficult. Wherever your business stands, optimizing the technical processes so that your sales and marketing team can have access to CRM and email data and be able use that data for marketing efforts will be necessary to effectively manage prospects, leads, and customers.

With so many platforms and options out there, there's no one-size-fits-all solution. The solution that's right for your business will depend on technology, budget, resource, and volume considerations. But no matter what you choose, you should be focused on having a fully integrated data process so that CRM and email data can work together and help you reach your business goals.

Data Integration Goals:

- Seamlessly integrate tools, so data is synchronized between the CRM and email marketing platforms. That way CRM data can influence email marketing activity, and the data from email marketing activity can be referenced and applied for CRM efforts.
- Use email and CRM data to learn more about a contact's preferences and behavior, and then use that data to strengthen and deepen the relationship.
- Keep your business goals in mind. Work toward having a system in place that combines and strengthens existing business processes while making it efficient for your employees.

Winner's Circle
- Before using your email marketing data for a campaign, cleanse the data by checking for formatting errors and other data-entry issues.
- Validate newly collected email marketing data by running it through a third-party verification platform.
- Make sure recipients can manage their own email marketing preferences to ensure they receive the messaging and frequency they desire.
- Optimize your data management process by establishing synchronization and automation within or between data platforms.
- Use marketing data to learn recipients' preferences and behaviors, and use that data to strengthen marketing relationships.

CHAPTER 8
Deliverability and Authentication

Starting Line

In this chapter you will learn:
- Why email sender reputation is more important than ever
- How data management can affect email deliverability
- How ISPs use honeypot and recycled email addresses
- What email authentication is and why you should use it
- How recipient engagement affects email deliverability

One of the biggest challenges for email marketers, whether B2B or B2C, is how to get their messages into a subscriber's inbox. Because email delivery rules are established by the receiving email server, they change depending on the ISP or business. And the differences can vary dramatically.

Over the past few years, reaching the inbox has become increasingly difficult. Even legitimate marketers sending legitimate messages may find their inbox placement rates continue to decline as email servers become more and more stringent about the messages they allow through to the inboxes of their users or employees.

Years ago, email message content was largely responsible for identifying spammers. Today, email deliverability is largely based on your reputation as a sender and less about the content of your messages. Content is still considered, but your sending practices are more important than ever.

STAT 22% of permission email never reaches the inbox, and another 4% ends up in subscribers' spam or junk folders.[36]

So how can you reduce the potential for your email to land in the junk, bulk, or spam folder? You can incorporate or implement several best practices to ensure the best-possible chance for your email to reach its intended destination. Those include maintaining clean data, using email authentication, and generating engagement.

Maintain Clean Data

Keeping clean data is more important than ever. Sending to a high percentage of bad or invalid addresses or sending to "honeypot" or "spam trap" addresses is a sign to receiving mail servers that you don't properly manage your data or that you use non-permission based data collection processes.

1. Remove invalid email addresses. One of the first things a receiving mail server looks for in a spam email is if it is being sent to a large number of invalid email addresses. Because spammers attempt to send to various name combinations at popular domains, a large amount of email to non-existing addresses usually raises concern that a message may be spam.

In order to combat this, marketers need to minimize the amount of email they are sending to bad addresses. Due to frequent changes in user data, it's impossible to reduce bad addresses completely. However, as long as the percentage of bad addresses is low, marketers should have acceptable inbox placement rates. So how can you reduce invalid email addresses? As mentioned in the previous chapter, cleanse and validate your email data and allow users the ability to update their information in a preference center.

2. Avoid spam traps. Spam-trap email addresses are set up to catch spammers. They are generally email addresses that exist only to receive email and have never been used to send it. Additionally, spam-trap emails do not engage with the email they receive, so they will not register opens or clicks.

Many spammers will try different combinations of popular names and naming techniques to guess at email addresses. When they send an email to a spam-trap address, it will receive it, so the sender believes it to be valid. These addresses are then used over and over again, and in many cases will be included in email lists that marketers purchase.

There are two types of spam trap addresses: honeypots and recycled addresses.

Honeypot addresses are email addresses that are created and published on websites. Spammers that scan the web to harvest email addresses will unknowingly include these honeypot addresses in their data collection. When they send to these addresses, the receiver knows that the data has been collected without permission and will mark those messages as spam.

A **recycled address** is an email address that was once active and then due to abandonment or non-use was closed for a period of time and re-activated at a later date. The inbox messages are then monitored, and anyone sending to that email address may be flagged as a potential spammer or at least a marketer who is not managing their data effectively. Someone sending to a recycled address has not been removing bad or inactive records from their data files or has purchased a list with recycled addresses included.

3. Avoid blacklists. A blacklist is a report that includes the names, domains, and/or IPs of senders that send unsolicited email. The blacklist is typically publicly listed on an Internet site, so others may reference it as a way to identify and fight spammers. Many ISPs and businesses use the blacklists as a reference and filter out messages from senders included on blacklist reports.

Legitimate marketers are rarely found on a blacklist, but marketers who send questionable messages to questionable lists may find themselves included, and that can lead to serious deliverability issues. For example, Gmail uses the blacklist Spamhaus, and any marketer on the Spamhaus blacklist will find that the majority of their messages will not be delivered to their subscribers' Gmail inbox.[37]

Incorporate Email Authentication

Many email services like Outlook, Yahoo! Mail, and Gmail, as well as many businesses, use authentication. Authentication is a process where a receiving email server will verify that a sender is authentic. Because many spammers will not set up authentication, an authenticated sender is more likely to be legitimate and, therefore, sending legitimate emails.

For email receivers, ensuring a valid identity is a good first step in determining the origin of the email, but it does not take into consideration any email history or reputation or determine if the email is trustworthy.

The most popular types of email authentication include DKIM, SPF and DMARC.

DKIM Authentication

Originally called Domain Keys, DKIM has emerged as the most popular email authentication system. When DKIM is set up by your system administrator, the sending email server adds a DKIM signature to the outgoing email. This signature is a string generated by encrypting parts of the email with a private key. When the email is received, the receiving server queries the domain of the email for the public key to decrypt the signature. If the decrypted information matches those parts of the email that were encrypted, the email is authenticated.

SPF Authentication

Sender Policy Framework (SPF) is an email validation process that verifies a sender. The receiving mail server will check that an incoming message from a domain is being sent from a host authorized by that domain's administrators. A domain administrator will publish their authorized sending hosts in their Domain Name System (DNS) records. Because spammers will forge their sending addresses, a check for a published SPF record to see if a sender is authorized is one way to separate legit messages from potential spam messages.

DMARC Authentication

Domain-based Message Authentication, Reporting & Conformance (DMARC) expands on the DKIM and SPF authentication methods. It allows senders to indicate that their emails are protected by DKIM and/or SPF, and informs the receiver on how to handle the message if neither of those authentication methods passes (for example, to reject the email or to put in bulk/junk folder). DMARC limits the receiver's exposure to potentially harmful messages by removing the guesswork on how they should handle messages that fail authentication. DMARC will also report back to the sender about messages that pass or fail authentication.

One of the issues with email authentication is that there's no agreed-upon industry standard, and because the pros and cons are different for each method, you can't rely on a receiving ISP or business to employ them. As an email sender, it is advised to set up authentication for each type before beginning your deliveries. That way your delivery history will start strong, and you'll achieve higher sender reputation scores.

Engagement Matters

How your recipients respond to your emails is becoming a major factor in deliverability. Many ISPs and businesses that receive email monitor whether or not a recipient opens and clicks on an email message. Opens and clicks usually mean a message is legitimate, as it is receiving positive attention. The larger IPSs (including Yahoo!, Gmail, and Outlook) have stated that they analyze which emails create engagement with their users through opens and clicks. Emails without engagement may be removed from the main inbox and end up in spam or bulk folders.

With this in mind it's more important than ever for marketers to tailor email content to the audience and deliver relevant, meaningful messages that generate engagement. Engagement not only is important to the overall success of your message but also may impact whether or not someone sees your message in the first place.

Winner's Circle
- Maintaining clean data is more important than ever. Including large percentages of bad addresses or including honeypot or recycled addresses will have a negative effect on the delivery of your message and may get it labeled as bulk or spam.
- Incorporating email authentication is one of the best ways to legitimize your email delivery and separate your messages from potential spam. At minimum, it is recommended that marketers set up SPF and DKIM authentication.
- In order to stay in the inbox, marketers must generate engagement with their messaging through opens and clicks.

PART THREE:
The Message: What You Need to Know

CHAPTER 9
B2B Emails Don't Have to Be Boring

Starting Line

In this chapter you will learn:
- Why you need a properly designed email
- What unique design challenges exist for B2B email marketers
- How to design your copy

Most B2B email campaigns play it too safe when it comes to design. In many cases, email creative is mundane, the layout is underwhelming, and there's a lack of visual appeal.

Just because marketers are emailing on behalf of a corporation, does that mean they can't impress recipients with their creative? Certainly not. But many marketers feel that as long as it looks "good enough" then it won't backfire.

Even within the parameters of corporate brand guidelines, there exists a way to improve the visual appeal of B2B email campaigns. Using more interesting graphics and photos, using more interesting colors, and improving the layout of your text can make your emails stand out from the rest of the play-it-safe campaigns in a recipient's inbox.

But good design doesn't just create a "wow" factor. It also serves a purpose. By creating visual interest, readers will spend more time with a message, which leads to higher levels of engagement. Humans process images 60,000 times faster than text[38], so using imagery that supports text and moves readers through the important parts of the email will yield better results.

TAKEAWAY

A properly designed email will not only capture attention but also highlight key messages and lead the reader to take a desired action. And the more often a message can get recipients to take action, the better chance there will be for increased conversions.

CASE STUDY

Indiemark: The World's Worst Email

Does design matter? Of course it does. But what happens when you try to make something stand out by intentionally making it ugly? Indiemark, an email marketing agency, attempted to find out.

PART THREE: The Message: What You Need To Know

Indiemark created the "World's Worst Email" and sent it to a segment of subscribers who work in the email marketing industry or have responsibility for email marketing for their business. The email, being about as ugly as ugly gets, ended up having lower than average opens and click rates, and ended up in the spam folder due to ignoring many best practices. The takeaway? Design matters. It is an extension of your brand, and it reinforces brand image. If you send a bad-looking email, it will instantly turn off your recipients and likely result in low open and click rates. Indiemark proved this by sending a great-looking promotional email to the same list a week later, and the results were nearly double the opens and triple the clicks.

This case study was originally prepared by Scott Hardigree for Email Critic. View the entire case study at http://b2bemailmarketingbook.com/resources.

Many times B2B emails have challenges that do not exist in the B2C marketing world. Here are some unique challenges that B2B marketers tend to face.

1. I have a lot of copy. Yes, many B2B emails need to have more than a special offer or a promotion like our B2C counterparts. We frequently have several paragraphs of content to deal with. So what do you do with copy to make it more interesting? You think about your copy the way you do any other visual element. Make it look attractive.

2. All I have is copy. That may be all that is provided to you, but that doesn't prevent you from grabbing a quality stock photograph, making a chart, or having your creative team design an image or graphic that supports the copy and message. Visual interest can also be created with your header, calls to action, and footer, and by adding small flourishes to your content area. Even small details like using dots instead of a line to separate content can make your email visually unique.

3. It's part of a print or direct mail campaign. An email is not a print campaign. An email is not a website. An email is not a direct mail piece. So don't treat it like one.

4. We've always done it this way. It's amazing how tradition can lock marketers into a feeling that they have to stick with the same old creative. Just because you've established a look and feel doesn't mean it's an effective look and feel. Make a change. Be bold. Do something different. Then see how your audience reacts. Did you get more click-throughs? Fewer unsubscribes? More conversions?

Design Your Copy

No one reads anymore, at least not in their email inbox or on the web. People can read, but many choose not too. There's simply not enough time to read everything we receive. We're trained to search for what we want and avoid what we don't. So how can marketers use this to their advantage? The answer is to **craft content for those that scan or skim their email messages.** So how can you design your copy for the scanners and skimmers? Here are some tips.

1. Make it scannable. Email recipients seldom read every word in an email from top to bottom. The majority of readers (80%) scan emails for content that catches their attention[39], and then they dig into the content if that message matches their interests. Prepare your email so that the key messages stand out. Allow people to find what they want to learn more about. Draw their eye to content and offers that they will find interesting.

2. Use headers and subheaders. Headers and subheaders serve several purposes. Besides offering a visual break in the copy, they also help readers understand what content will be presented in the following copy. If readers want, they can then skip a section and move on to the next without feeling like they're wasting their time with content they already know or understand.

3. Break apart the copy. Large blocks of copy in giant paragraphs are a visual turnoff to most readers. Upon seeing them, many will even dismiss your email. If an email looks boring, readers will assume it will be boring. And that's not the signal you want to suggest from the layout of your copy. Keep your copy short. Keep it on point. Avoid long paragraphs. Break the copy into smaller chunks or segments.

4. Use bullets and lists. Using lists and bullet points is a great way to break up content. So how can bullets and lists help?
- They're a natural draw for readers.
- They create an easy way to present multiple points.
- They are easily scannable.
- They provide a visual break for readers.

5. Use bold and italics. Proper use of **bold** and *italic* typefaces can help you **stress key points** and **highlight important messages** by providing visual elements that catch the eye's attention, thereby delivering the *most important parts of your message*.

6. Use font size variations. When appropriate, use different font sizes for different elements of copy. Headers, subheaders, and body copy can all be slightly different, which will provide more of a visual break for readers and help you make your most important messages more visible.

7. Use color. The best content in the world can look boring when presented in black and white. So use color to your advantage. Pick a color scheme for your messages, and use color for headers, subheaders, links, and backgrounds. While using color almost always produces more interesting visuals than black and white, color can also be overused or used improperly. Always make sure your message is readable, and don't use color to the point where it becomes a distraction.

8. Use whitespace. What you leave blank can be as important as what you don't leave blank. Make sure your message doesn't feel crowded. Allow for space between lines, between sections of content, in the margins, etc. To test if you have enough whitespace, simply look at your message. If it feels friendly and inviting, you're probably in good shape. If it looks bulky or uninviting, try to spend more time with your formatting.

Winner's Circle
- Good email design leads readers to take action. Spend time testing designs to see what resonates best with your recipients.
- Make your email scannable. Make sure readers can quickly review the email and find what interests them.
- Make your copy look attractive. Break it up into smaller fragments. Add headers and subheaders. Then use bullets, bold, italics, font variations, color, and whitespace to make it scannable.

PART THREE: The Message: What You Need To Know

CHAPTER 10
Copywriting and Tonality

Starting Line

In this chapter you will learn:
- How to best prepare copy for your email campaigns
- How email is experienced in stages, and how to prepare copy for all stages
- What tactics to employ for preparing the from name, subject line, and preheader
- What winning strategies to employ for subject lines
- What copywriting tactics to apply for the email body
- Why landing pages must be an extension of the email

Writing email copy is a difficult task. Finding the exact words and phrases that will perform best with your target audience is easier said than done. What may speak well to one recipient may not make an impression on another. The challenge is to find what language works best, and try to keep it fresh and interesting from campaign to campaign.

One of the biggest pitfalls for B2B email copywriters is that they construct their message copy from their business point of view. Their only concern is delivering an intended message or offer. So they fail to consider what the recipient wants to receive.

Messages filled with self-promotional content, corporate information, and business-heavy content like news articles and press releases is seldom what recipients are looking for from their business connections.

What's in It for Me?

Putting yourself in the position of your recipient is key to delivering a relevant message. Answering the age-old question "What's in it for me?" will help you create better email content. If you don't deliver content that can save users time, save them money, or provide relevant information, then they most likely won't read, won't take action on your message, or may even unsubscribe.

TAKEAWAY

Not delivering relevant content to your audience is the biggest mistake made by email marketers.

TAKEAWAY

Your email copy must be relevant to the recipient, and it must deliver value.

PART THREE: The Message: What You Need To Know

Email Is Experienced in Stages

The success of an email campaign starts at the recipient's inbox. The inbox, being the first experience the user will have with your email, is stage one. The stage one content has to be relevant enough to move the user to stage two, which is the email message itself. The email message must then generate enough interest to encourage an action, which is typically a click to a website or landing page, which is stage three.

Thinking about your campaign in three stages will help you understand how important each stage is to the success of your campaign. You have to move the recipient through these three stages in order to generate a conversion, which is likely your ultimate goal. So understanding the three stages of email is key to reaching your marketing objectives.

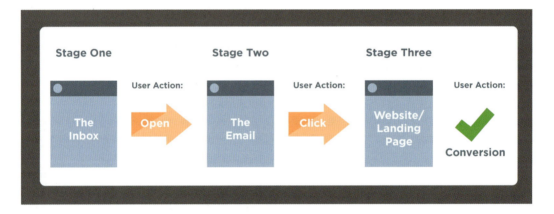

Stage One: The Inbox

When a recipient receives an email they will typically make a quick decision about whether they want to read it immediately, save it for later, or delete it. Their decision is made based on the three things they see in the inbox (prior to even seeing the body of the message). Most email software will display the following:

1. The from name
2. The subject line
3. The preheader

If a recipient feels that this information meets their interests, they'll move on to viewing your email either in their preview window or as a full message. If the inbox content doesn't resonate, your email will likely be deleted.

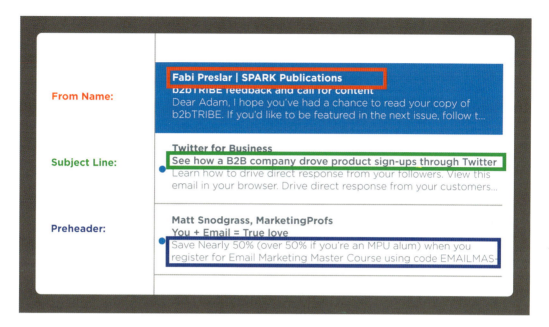

When developing email messages, many marketers concentrate on the email exclusively without giving due attention to these initial items. Don't make that mistake. Understand that you must make a connection in the inbox to even get to the point where a recipient views your email message.

The From Name

The from name is simply the sender's name, whether that's a business or a person. In nearly all cases, the from name will appear in the recipient inbox, and it is usually the first item the recipient will see. Best practices for the from name include:

1. Test using the business name or personal name. To start, default to using the business name unless the recipient has an established relationship with the sender or if the sender name is easily recognized and tied to the brand (think Richard Branson, who doesn't need to say, "CEO of Virgin Group of Companies"). However, some tests have shown that creating a personal connection by using a person's name achieves a lift in open rates. Test using the business name, a person's name, or both, and see what works best for you.

2. Don't exceed 23 characters. Recipients on the most popular mobile devices will typically see the first 23 characters of the from name. If your from name is longer than that, make sure it's easy to identify if you extend beyond the mobile limitation. Desktop and webmail clients will display more characters (typically around 50 to 75), so your entire from name will likely display in those environments.

PART THREE: The Message: What You Need To Know

3. Be consistent. Use the same from name consistently, so recipients learn to recognize your emails. If you create a positive experience for them, they'll seek out your messages, or at least save them to read later. Changing your from name repeatedly will prevent this from happening and will generate confusion.

4. Be very consistent. You should be consistent not only with the from name but also with the from email. Why? Because users might whitelist you by adding you to their contact list or safe sender list. Changing your from email could be the difference between being in the inbox with images on or being in the spam folder.

The Subject Line

The subject line is the first impression you'll make with the marketing message of your email. It's usually the first significant factor in the success of your email campaign.

The goal of a subject line is to not only capture the attention of the prospect with an appealing idea or offer but also to convert their attention into interest. Your subject line should be the first catalyst toward starting a process of action, which usually begins with the recipient opening the email.

Because you want your subject line to be easily understood, never use a subject line that the recipient has to decipher or make a connection to understand. A reader should never have to stop, pause, or think about a subject line. It must be easily and instantly understood.

Some examples of good subject lines:

Sender: American Express
Subject Line: Smart business tips you don't want to miss
Why it's a good subject line: simple, invokes curiosity

Sender: GE Reports
Subject Line: Light My Sleigh Tonight: The Story of Rudolph and GE
Why it's a good subject line: creates interest, seasonally topical

Sender: PreGel America
Subject Line: Only 4 Days Left to Save 15% on Hot Summer Flavors!
Why it's a good subject line: creates urgency, provides incentive

In order to have a successful subject line you'll need to consider not only your marketing message but also the technical limitations of how it is displayed. So consider these winning strategies for subject lines.

Winning Subject Line Strategy #1: Put the Main Point First

The area in a prospect's inbox that displays the subject line usually has limited space; therefore, subject lines tend to perform better when they are point-first. Start your subject line with the offer, and then use the remaining space to support it.

Winning Subject Line Strategy #2: Create Interest

Your goal for your subject line is to stand out in the inbox and generate action from the recipients. Some tactics that have shown success for B2B marketers include numeric lists, for example "7 Ways To X" or "Top 10 Reasons to X." "How to" subject lines also usually fare well, for example "How To Reduce Inbound Support Calls" or "How To Increase Quality Leads." These work because they create curiosity and generate interest, which result in the recipient opening the email.

Winning Subject Line Strategy #3: Create Urgency

People don't want to miss out on something important, so use that to your advantage. Subject lines that create urgency tend to generate immediate interest. Including an urgent timeframe such as "1 day left to register" or mentioning limited availability such as "5 seats left for our next event" is effective for spurring action from your recipients.

Winning Subject Line Strategy #4: Listen and Respond

Listen to clients and customers. Learn what issues and challenges they face. Then craft a subject line that addresses those concerns. Generate opens by answering the questions your recipients are already asking.

Winning Subject Line Strategy #5: Test Length

Marketers who have tested subject line length have found that shorter subject lines tend to lead to higher open rates, while longer subject lines produce more click-throughs. Perhaps curiosity sparked by shorter subject lines creates interest, driving opens, while longer subject lines better explains the email content, resulting in

PART THREE: The Message: What You Need To Know

better click-through rates but lower opens. In any case, subject line length can affect the results of your campaign. Test both short and very long subject lines to see how they perform for you.

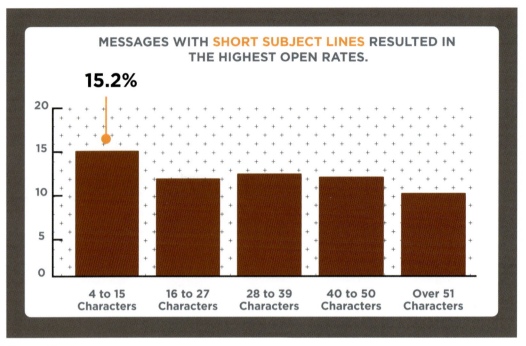

Shorter subject lines attract attention and lead to slightly higher open rates.

Winning Subject Line Strategy #6: Test Your Keywords

Certain keywords in subject lines generate more interest than others. For B2B emails, studies have shown that news terms such as "breaking," "alert," and "bulletin" achieved better than average results, while discount terms such as "free," "save," and "half price" didn't do so well. Content terms such as "top stories" did well, but benefit terms including "special" and "exclusive" did not.

In the end, you'll only know what works for you by testing. Set up A/B tests on your subject lines to see which one your audience prefers. Continue to refine and test, and then deliver the best performing subject lines to the majority of your list.

Winning Subject Line Strategy #7: Beware Personalization

Adding personalization to a subject line may seem like a good tactic, but results can be mixed. Results have shown that personalization can help achieve a higher open rate, but fail when it comes to click-throughs. Again, testing is always recommended, but don't expect subject line personalization to lead to an improvement in your campaign results.

Winning Subject Line Strategy #8: Use Clear Language

Use language that is clear, succinct, and easy to understand. Do not use gimmicks, plays on words, or other "gotcha" tactics like link-bait subject lines or implying an offer that's not actually redeemable.

Do NOT do these things in your subject line:
1. Use multiple exclamation points. It looks spammy and will reduce your open rates.
2. USE ALL CAPS. It makes subject lines difficult to read and comes across as loud and obnoxious.
3. Be vague. Clarity will get you opens. Being vague will get you deleted.
4. Be tricky. Trying to get an increase in opens by starting your email with a "FW:" or "RE:" could reduce your open rates by over 40%.[40]

The Preheader

A preheader is a short text summary that displays after the subject line when an email is viewed in the inbox. It is taken from the first lines of copy found in email. Many mobile, desktop, and web email clients provide preheaders to tip users off on what the email contains before they open it. They're helpful to the recipient and, therefore, important to the marketer.

In most email clients, the preheader is shown next to or underneath the subject line in the viewer's inbox. If images aren't turned on, the preheader will still appear, acting as an excerpt of what the email is about.

Here's a wonderful preheader from an email from Litmus to its customers.

> **Litmus**   2:37PM
> **Email Design Monthly: Gmail's spam rule + Dreamweaver snippets**
> Articles we love about things we love. In an email about email. #someta Email Design Monthly An infrequent digest of curated email & design articles from Litmus with ♥ ...

And here's the email. Notice the preheader shows the opening text and the start of the body text.

PART THREE: The Message: What You Need To Know

Most of the time, the only preheader recipients see is "Don't Miss Our Emails..." or "View Online" because most marketers start their emails with that kind of language. They don't take advantage of using a preheader. That's a big mistake. And although I enjoy receiving the MultiView email newsletter every Friday, this is an example of not taking advantage of an email preheader:

MultiView Inc. 4:00PM
Internet users send 204 million emails per minute
This message contains images. If you don't see images, click here to view. Advertise in this news brief. Text version   RSS   Subscribe   Unsubscribe...

A proper preheader will introduce the content of the email in a quick, short phrase that ideally will capture the viewer's interest. Use a preheader to summarize the email, provide a call-to-action, generate interest, or give your users a reason to open the full message.
This example from Staples shows how a subject line and a preheader can work well together to create urgency and provide a savings incentive.

> **Staples Promotional Products**   7:06PM
> **This coupon is hot. Act fast!**
> 25% off + free shipping. Buy Now View this offer in your web browser. Forward this offer to a friend. May 2nd - June 5th Start saving now. • Increase brand aw...

Preheader Copywriting Strategies

There are several ways to make a preheader work for your email. Which one you choose depends on your brand, the email you're sending, and most importantly, your audience.

1. Provide a call to action. Your preheader text can provide a call to action, just like a button or link in the email. Example: Register for next month's conference today and save 25%.

2. Generate interest. Give users something intriguing so they want to open the email. Example: What are you waiting for? You have to see these new products.

3. Summarize. Provide a summary, so users know that this is an important email from a trusted brand. Your reader should recognize your brand from the sender name and should see something they know, something that resonates. Example: Software update, new features, free download.

4. Always support the subject line. No matter what you write for your preheader, never repeat the subject line, and make sure your preheader supports the subject line content. It should act as a subheadline or play off the subject line message.
If you combine an action-oriented, specific preheader with a winning subject line, you could significantly increase your email campaign open rates.

TAKEAWAY

When a preheader is used in conjunction with the subject line in a way that complements or adds detail to the subject line message, it can create a powerful message prior to the reader even opening the email.

Stage Two: The Email Body

Marketers who adopt a tone that resonates with readers will have an advantage over their competition. So how do you write effective email copy? And what do you need to do to craft a message

PART THREE: The Message: What You Need To Know

that resonates? These copywriting tactics are regularly found in successful email campaigns.

Winning Copywriting Tactic #1:
Imagine yourself as the recipient and write to persuade yourself.

Do you talk to your customers or talk at them? Does your copy resonate or alienate?

TIP

Write your copy with your recipients in mind. Put yourself in their shoes, and think about what they want to hear.

Winning Copywriting Tactic #2:
Start with the benefit.

At a time when inbox volume continues to grow, readers have less and less time to spend scouring through their messages. You have to make an impact fast, and it has to be obvious to the reader why they should take action on your message.

One thing to avoid is beginning emails with a personal introduction or otherwise meaningless copy. This offers no value.

Winning Copywriting Tactic #3:
Be helpful.

Are you coming across as being sales-y or helpful?

TAKEAWAY

If you can't persuade yourself, you won't be able to persuade your target audience either.

Not sure how to be helpful? Think about the last few questions your customers asked. Or talk with your support or service team and ask them what questions they are asked regularly. Ask for input from your staff or coworkers. You can also learn from your customers, either directly or through a poll or survey.

And if none of those are options, check your website traffic or search marketing for trends in what your visitors are accessing, and provide more information on those topics.

Winning Copywriting Tactic #4:
Lead the recipient toward a decision.

TIP

When you lead with a benefit, readers will instantly know why your message will help them address a core business value: saving time, saving money, or providing valuable educational content.

The goal of effective email copy is to serve a recipient in a way that enables them to quickly make the best decision. To make the best decision, a recipient must be able to understand and accept a series of logical premises that lead them to take action on the message, which usually comes in the form of a click-through.

How To Win At B2B Email Marketing

This email from Twitter is a good example of succinct copywriting that leads to action. It states the desired action (give feedback), a benefit (take the survey to redeem $100 in Twitter Ads), and leads the recipient to click (Let's go!).

TAKEAWAY

Readers always respond better to messages that inform and educate.

TAKEAWAY

Whatever you do, don't oversell. Teach and then sell. If you are helpful and educate, then the sale will come to you.

TIP

Write your copy so that it leads the recipient to CLICK. Your email copy should be long enough to sell the click, but no longer.

Winning Copywriting Tactic #5: Make it a dialogue.

Your email message should be conversational. People don't buy from emails. People buy from people. Use email copy to make a personal connection, as opposed to using blatant personalization to make it feel like you're speaking to someone. Ask for the participation of your reader and encourage your audience to continue the conversation in other channels.

PART THREE: The Message: What You Need To Know

Winning Copywriting Tactic #6: Make it long enough, but no longer.

Your email copy should be long enough to get across the main point of your message, and no longer. Too little or too much copy can reduce your response rate. It has been found that if you want to achieve a click-through, the ideal length of an email is between 300 to 500 characters.[41] Therefore, email marketers should focus on being direct with their content and calls-to-action.

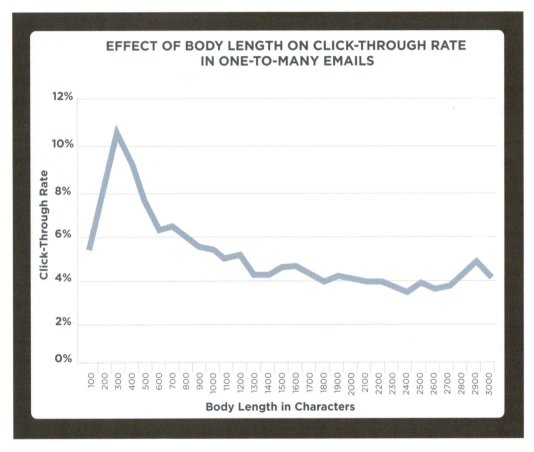

EFFECT OF BODY LENGTH ON CLICK-THROUGH RATE IN ONE-TO-MANY EMAILS

Messages with shorter body length lead to increased click-through rate. If you review your email and recognize that certain parts of it do not lead toward your goal, delete that part of the copy. If it's unnecessary, don't burden your reader with the extra content.

Also, keep your paragraphs or other blocks of copy as short as possible. Visually, long paragraphs are a turn-off to readers. Don't make reading your message feel like a chore. Convey your key point and benefits in short, clear, easy-to-read segments.

Stage Three:
The Landing Page or Website

A user's email experience doesn't end at the inbox. A seamless connection from email to website or landing page is essential for driving action and conversions. If there's a disconnect between the email experience and what happens after the click, chances are you'll lose readers' interest or create a frustrating user experience.

A winning landing page needs to be an extension of the email. It should feel like a progression and provide a clear path of action for conversion.

This example from ON24 (see next page) shows an email with a link to a webinar registration and the landing page for registering. The email copy and design is consistent from email to landing page, making it easy for a recipient to click through and convert.

By doing so, you'll be able to gauge how you want your email copy to flow into the landing page and what copy will help move the user from email to conversion.

Write your email and landing page copy simultaneously. By doing so, you keep a similar writing style throughout, and make sure your landing page follows up on everything you promise in your email.

TIP

When writing emails that convert at a landing page, try writing your email and landing page at the same time.

PART THREE: The Message: What You Need To Know

Adam,

Webinars have become the most important tool for marketers to generate new leads and drive demand. To achieve these goals, you need a platform that is built to drive your marketing programs. Attend ON24's upcoming webcast "**7 Signs You Need to Reevaluate Your Webinar Platform**," and hear Patrick Bruner, JOICO Communications Project Manager, explain how to select the right webinar platform.

In this webinar you will hear:

- Differences between conferencing tools and webcasting platforms
- Key webinar features that are essential to marketers
- A live customer case study on choosing the right webinar platform
- Keys to engaging webinar audiences

Register now

REGISTER NOW

Overview

Title 7 Signs You Need to Reevaluate Your Webinar Platform

Date Wednesday, July 23

Time 11:00 AM PT / 2:00 PM ET

Duration 45 minutes plus live Q&A

Speakers

Mark Bornstein
Senior Director,
Content Marketing
ON24, Inc.

Patrick Bruner
Communications
Project Manager
JOICO

Contact Us | Visit Us | Privacy Policy
Copyright ©2014 ON24 Inc. All Rights Reserved

To unsubscribe from future e-mails or to update your e-mail preferences, click here.
ON24, Inc.
201 Third Street, 3rd Floor | San Francisco, CA 94103 | 877.202.9599
Privacy Policy

7 SIGNS YOU NEED TO REEVALUATE YOUR WEBINAR PLATFORM

Webinars have become the most important tool for marketers to generate new leads and drive demand. You can't afford to use a platform that isn't built to drive your marketing programs. Attend "7 Signs That You Need to Reevaluate Your Webinar Platform" and learn about the key features and functionality that make webinars powerful marketing tools.

In this interactive webinar, you will learn:

- Differences between conference tools and webcasting platforms
- Key webinar features that are essential to marketers
- A live customer case study on choosing the right webinar platform
- Keys to engaging webinar audiences

SPEAKERS

Mark Bornstein
Senior Director, Content Marketing
ON24, Inc.

As Sr. Director of Content Marketing for ON24, Mark manages content strategy and marketing communications in support of webcasting and virtual events solutions. Mark brings over 20 years of content marketing, account management and communications experience with leading technology firms, including: Cisco, GE Access and Compatible Systems.

Patrick Bruner
Communications Project Manager
JOICO

Patrick Bruner has worked in the corporate beauty industry since 1995, first with Aveda Corporation, then Estee Lauder Companies and since 2008 with Shiseido Corporation's Joico division as their Communications Project Manager. At Shiseido's Joico division he has a wide range of responsibilities, but most importantly is charged with upgrading the company's digital outreach to the beauty professional and consumer.

If you have already registered for this webcast, click here>>

Copyright © 2014 ON24 Inc. Home | Solutions | Products | Partners | Company | Contact Us | Careers | Privacy Policy

OVERVIEW

TITLE: 7 Signs You Need to Reevaluate Your Webinar Platform
DATE: Wednesday, July 23
TIME: 11:00 am PT | 2:00 pm ET
DURATION: 45 minutes plus live Q&A

REGISTER NOW

First Name*
Last Name*
Company*
Email Address*
Business Phone*
Title*

REGISTER NOW

Winner's Circle:

- Your email copy must be relevant to the recipient and must deliver value.
- In order to create a conversion, you first must create an open and then a click. Consider how recipients will get from an open to a click then to the landing page or website.
- You have to earn the open by using a trusted from name along with a compelling subject line and preheader.
- Write your copy with your recipients in mind. Put yourself in their shoes and consider what they want to hear.
- Lead your email with the benefit, and make it clear what action you want readers to take.
- Don't oversell. Be human. Create a dialogue.
- Only make your copy as long as it needs to be and no longer.
- Your landing page or website should be an extension of the email. It needs to be a seamless experience in order to generate a conversion.

PART THREE: The Message: What You Need To Know

CHAPTER 11
Content: What Really Matters

Starting Line

In this chapter you will learn:
- Why generating quality content will lead to better marketing results
- What winning tactics to employ to create quality email content
- How to generate B2B content ideas
- How to understand your audience

Quality content means more engaged subscribers, more interactions, more sharing, and ultimately, more conversions. Content creation requires time, budget, and resources, which always seem to be in short supply, and that's what makes it challenging for B2B email marketers.

So how do you create quality email content?

Winning Content Tactic #1: Don't sell. Educate.

The last thing you want to receive in your inbox is a blatant promotional message where the only message is a sales pitch. There's no value for the recipient; the sender is only thinking of their best interests.

When you provide educational material that informs, enlightens, or provides insight, you are delivering value to your readers. Readers will consider your emails helpful, and that will create a positive brand experience. And when recipients have a positive connection with your brand, that will be top of mind when they're ready to take action.

So when it comes time to recommend a brand for a purchase or other business relationship, which brand do you think email recipients will choose? The one that's been providing quality educational content or the one that's only been sending sales pitches?

> **TAKEAWAY**
>
> In order to be effective, email marketing must become more strategic, more trusted and more relevant. Brands that provide high quality content will become more trusted, and a brand that is more trusted will spark more engagement and realize better results.

PART THREE: The Message: What You Need To Know

Here's an email from Grainger that educates recipients on how to choose the right ladder. It works because it leads with educational content, and that knowledge can make recipients feel more secure that they are purchasing the best product for their needs.

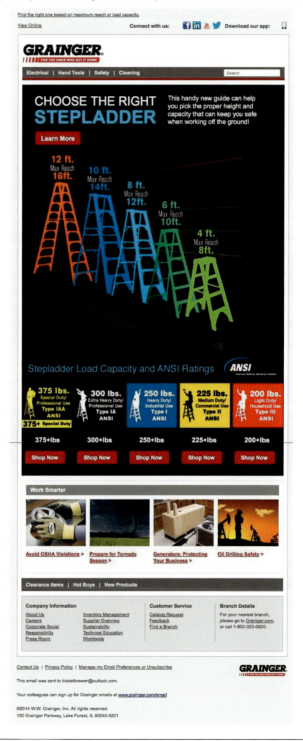

Winning Content Tactic #2: Solve a problem.

Everyone has challenges with his or her business. What can you or your organization do to help address these challenges? Does your product or service help solve common business problems?

Put yourself in the shoes of a subscriber. Would you sign up for an email newsletter that helps you solve your business problems? Most of us would.

Winning Content Tactic #3: Save. Save. Save.

People want to save money, save time, save resources, and save themselves from aggravation. What can you provide that will save your audience? Don't think savings only come in the form of a coupon. Reducing calls into customer support or the amount of manual labor required for a task are also major savings benefits to businesses.

Winning Content Tactic #4: Entertain.

When used appropriately, entertaining content can resonate well with your audience. At times, email can serve simply to provide enjoyment. And yes, B2B marketers are allowed to entertain their audiences. Some recipients will be even more receptive to emails if they stand out from their inbox full of mundane content. And after all, when people find your style entertaining, they'll keep coming back for more.

B2B Content Idea Starters

Coming up with ideas for quality content can be a challenge for any marketer. Finding what will resonate with your audience is key. Some types of content seem to consistently draw interest from recipients. Here are some ideas of types of content you can try in your B2B communications.

How-Tos, Tips & Lists
1. Tips & tricks
2. Step-by-step guides
3. Problems and solutions
4. Checklists

TAKEAWAY

A winning strategy is to begin with highlighting a problem your audience experiences and show how you can help solve it. There's no better way to make subscribers feel good about your brand than showing how you can address their biggest problems.

TIP

Showing your audience how to save is not just a tactic to be used pre-sale. Sharing ways your business can help people save is a great topic to cover in emails where the goals are retention and generating advocacy.

PART THREE: The Message: What You Need To Know

5. Lists (top 10)
6. Do's and don'ts
7. Debunking common myths

Business Content
8. Case studies
9. Customer testimonials
10. Interviews (written or video)
11. Frequently asked questions (FAQs) with answers
12. Product or service reviews
13. Polls or surveys
14. Photos from business events or internal operations
15. Videos (behind the scenes, events, etc.)
16. Social media best-of (featuring the posts, tweets, etc. with the most feedback)
17. Slideshows
18. Infographics

Aggregated & Curated Content
19. Reference new research or a new study and feature its results.
20. Provide links to interesting industry content (just make sure it's not a competitor).
21. Review an event (conference, webinar, etc.) and provide a recap or takeaways.
22. Review other content and provide your analysis.
23. Recap your most popular content.

Think outside the inbox. Remember that your recipients are not likely aware of all the content that you post on your blog, in social media, and on your website. Sharing these items in your email will ensure that you maximize the impact of what you've created and ensure that your connections are becoming aware of your content from multiple channels.

TIP

When it comes to sourcing great content, don't be afraid to re-purpose the content from your blog or website. And don't be afraid to re-use or update old content if it is still relevant.

Know Your Audience

In order to provide the most relevant marketing content, you have to understand your audience: their likes, dislikes, pain points, and challenges. Anticipating who will be reading your message is key to producing effective content. Plan your content from their perspective.

Ask yourself these questions to see how much you understand about your audience.

1. What do they want? What is it that they are looking for from you? Do you provide something they want? If so, are you giving that to them?

2. What don't they want? What topics should you avoid? What do you think is an instant turn-off? Is anything you plan to include potentially controversial or harmful to your business or your professional reputation?

3. Why are you connected? What benefit or potential solution do you bring to the table that warranted them to reach out and connect with you in the first place?

4. What issues are they facing? Everyone has a problem or issue. How can you provide a solution?

5. How can you solve their problem? What do you bring to the table that is unique, helpful, and beneficial to your audience?

6. What do you want them to do? Provide a clear path to your goal. Make it a singular objective. Do everything you can to drive them toward the one goal you want to achieve with each campaign.

7. What incentive will make them convert? Is there something valuable that you can provide that will incent the recipient to take action on your message and complete a conversion?

8. What may keep them from converting? Why would someone be unable to reach your goal? Can you prevent that from happening?

It's always important to put yourself in the mindset of your recipient. Think about how you would react to your email campaign if you were on the receiving end. Is it useful? Does it provide value? If you feel that your marketing is coming up short and not addressing the concerns or interests of your audience, you need to reconsider your approach and work to address any issues.

TAKEAWAY

Always keep your audience's best interests in mind. Deliver relevance. Provide value.

CASE STUDY

Exact Software: Using Data to Generate Custom Content

Business software supplier Exact Software uses profile data to present the most topical content in its email newsletters.

By using the data from the industry field in the profile of each recipient, Exact Software customizes its email newsletters to include industry-specific content and calls-to-action.

PART THREE: The Message: What You Need To Know

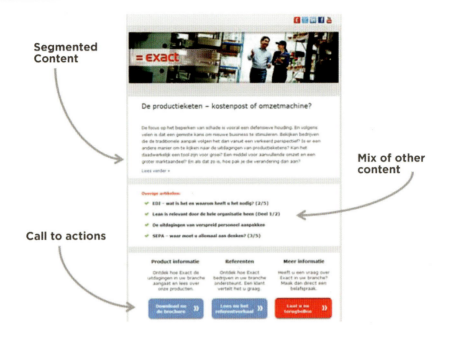

The calls-to-action, also being dynamic based on industry, are frequently changed based on existing or newer options like an industry-specific webinar.

Those without profile data receive a generic newsletter with a link to customize their news.

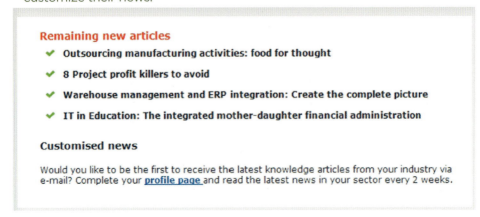

Recipients receive an email every two weeks. The activity from Exact Software's email marketing program enters into a lead scoring program. With that data, Exact Software can identify sales qualified leads in around four weeks. From all sales qualified leads, 42% turn into sales accepted leads, and of that, 20% are true opportunities. At this point, 4% of the opportunities have resulted in a deal. That number is expected to rise since the product has a long sales cycle.

This case study was originally prepared by Jordie van Rijn of eMail Monday. It was included in the Marketing Automation Best Practices Implementation Guide *by Smart Insights. This version has been edited to include key points of dynamic email content. View the entire case study at http://b2bemailmarketingbook.com/resources.*

Suggestions for Authentic B2B Communications

1. Be human. Yes, you hear this all the time. Be human. It's a widely known tactic ... that hardly anyone uses.

People are behind every B2B business. People do business with people. Be personal. Show some personality. Give your business contacts a reason to reach out and connect. Stop the corporate speak. Write your content the same way you talk to people. You'll be amazed at the change in reception and response.

2. Be passionate. Share the great things your business is doing, and be proud of your success. Let your audience know that you do great work and that you're passionate about your business, your products or services, your clients/customers, and your industry.

As long as you don't sound like you're bragging, being passionate will give your contacts a reason to take notice of your brand, and it'll create an emotional connection. Remember that people want to connect.

3. Be the expert, but seek feedback. It's great to engage with a wide variety of people and receive the advice they have to offer. After all, *you never learn when you're the one who's doing all the talking.*

Seeking feedback and advice from your audience can open up the communication channels and show the people behind the brand. Once you establish a professional personal connection, it's much easier to continue a conversation.

PART THREE: The Message: What You Need To Know

4. Everyone is your audience, even if they're not. You never know who might be your next client or customer. Even if you think someone isn't your target audience, *they are still your audience.* Don't ever discount the power of a positive brand experience, as people will change positions in their careers and provide referrals, all which may come back to you at some point.

So don't limit yourself to only talking to certain companies or managing connections outside your target audience. Those connections may turn out to be your best opportunities at a later date.

If you can genuinely connect with your audience through email marketing, you'll not only build a trusted relationship but also see success extend into other channels as well. If you continue to build that trusted relationship, you'll be the brand that rises to the top when it's time for the prospect to make a choice.

The best marketing doesn't feel like marketing at all. Create quality content and recipients will take notice, and you'll see winning results from your campaign efforts.

Winner's Circle

- High-quality content leads to increased trust, which leads to more engagement, which leads to more conversions.
- How do you create quality content? Educate recipients. Solve their problems. Save them time, money, or resources. Or entertain them.
- Find types of content that resonate with your audience. Don't be afraid to aggregate and curate existing content or content from other channels.
- Try to understand your audience. Consider what they want—their likes, dislikes, pain points, and challenges.
- Be human, be passionate, and be the expert, but always listen and seek feedback.

CHAPTER 12
The B2B Newsletter

Starting Line

In this chapter you will learn:
- How to set goals for B2B email newsletters
- Whether to prepare content for all audiences or to segment and use dynamic content
- Why you should put your content on your website and link newsletter readers to access full versions of it there
- How much of your content should be informational and how much should be promotional
- What not to do with your B2B email newsletter

Newsletters allow businesses to stay in touch with their existing relationships in a way that is efficient, affordable, and trackable. This is why many B2B businesses use them as the cornerstones of their email marketing efforts. The goals for most B2B newsletters tend to span a wide range of objectives, but for the most part B2B marketers want to:

1. Grow or strengthen brand awareness.
2. Establish thought leadership.
3. Educate recipients about the value of their products and services.
4. Strengthen existing relationships.
5. Retain and up-sell current customers.
6. Reduce customer churn.

Because newsletters are typically delivered to a wide audience, newsletter content should cover a wide range of material that is suitable for all audiences. Recipients tend to fall into one of several categories:

1. Someone who wants to stay in touch with your company
2. A prospective lead
3. An existing client or customer
4. A business partner or vendor

PART THREE: The Message: What You Need To Know

The challenge that newsletters present is trying to provide quality content that speaks to all recipients and works toward all business goals. Unless your business has a large list that it can segment into different audiences and has the resources to produce multiple newsletters, your newsletter will have the goal of providing interesting content for all your recipients.

> **STAT** Email newsletters generated 21.1% unique opens compared to 16.3% in promotional emails and 4.5% unique clicks compared to 2.8% in promotional emails.[42]

So how do you create quality B2B email newsletters?

Winning Newsletter Tactic #1: Select content that appeals to all audiences.

Some recipients will have little knowledge about your brand; others will be intimately familiar with everything you do. If you send the same newsletter to everyone, pick content like case studies, testimonials, educational materials, videos, and other items that will resonate with all readers.

Winning Newsletter Tactic #2: Segment and use dynamic content.

If you have a wide range of content and have the ability to segment your database between leads, customers, vendors, and other contacts, then prepare content for each audience. When you target a specific group, like "leads" or "existing customers," you can tailor your newsletter content to provide information that is most compelling to each group. Insert the various content dynamically so that you deliver the most relevant information to the reader.

TIP
Create a content hub, and link from your email newsletter to the content hub on your website.

Winning Newsletter Tactic #3: Get readers to your website.

Emails will come and go. Once deleted, email content may be lost forever. If you produce content for your email campaigns, maximize its value by putting it on your website.

Be sure that your content hub includes all your past and present email content, and make it searchable and sharable. This way you can continuously reference all the content you've created, and readers can easily find content from previous newsletters. You can also track which content is most popular and use your web analytics data to determine what topics are most interesting to your readers.

Winning Newsletter Tactic #4: Make it scannable.

Remember, people don't read email. They scan it. Make the important elements stand out. Design the content to allow your readers to visually jump from article to article to find what's most relevant to their interests.

Winning Newsletter Tactic #5: Produce subscriber-focused content.

People are subscribed to you for a reason—they like your brand and want to hear from you. So deliver value by providing subscriber-focused content. Give them information that will inform or educate. And make it enjoyable. If you give recipients helpful, relevant content, they'll look forward to receiving your newsletter and will share it with others. This brings more exposure, leads, and revenue-generating opportunities.

TIP

A lot of successful newsletter producers use the 80/20 rule: 80% of your content should be informational, while the remaining 20% can be promotional.

Winning Newsletter Tactic #6: Include some company news.

Your newsletter has to deliver value to the recipient, but that doesn't mean you can't fold in some corporate news and information.

According to a study by the Nielsen Norman group, 60% of email newsletter users rate a company news section as "valuable content."[43] This section keeps subscribers connected to your company. And when recipients feel more connected to a company, they are more likely to do business with them.

Winning Newsletter Tactic #7: Link away.

Your newsletter doesn't need to keep people in their inbox. Use links to push recipients to your website, social channels, content downloads, blog, etc. This may help you capture additional data and open additional connection methods (follows on social channels, subscriptions to blog posts, etc.). Each additional connection allows you to deepen your relationship and increase the number of touch points you have with each subscriber.

Winning Newsletter Tactic #8: Connect.

The whole point of your newsletter is to stay in touch with your contacts, so allow them to stay in touch with you. Make sure your newsletter comes from a real email address that will be monitored for replies, and ask recipients to reply to share their thoughts and feedback. And if they email you, respond back.

Remind recipients that people are behind the marketing and that they can reach out and connect. Also provide other forms of contact information, such as phone numbers, social channels, and a mailing address.

Winning Newsletter Tactic #9: Use behavioral data to influence decisions.

TIP
Review your analytics to find trends in what content draws interest.

Are recipients opening your email? Are they clicking on links? Which articles do people click on most? Use that information when deciding on what to prepare for future newsletters. Give the readers more of what they want.

Newsletters Reach Decision Makers

One of the benefits of email newsletters is that they reach decision makers. Business executives use email newsletters as a source for business information and industry news. A recent survey found that 60% of C-level executives, vice presidents, managing partners, and managing directors read an email newsletter as one of the first three news sources they check daily, while 56% of executives rely on email newsletters more than websites and general news sites as their primary source of industry news.[44]

And when it comes to sharing that information, decision makers use email more than any other channel; 80% share via email, while 43% use Twitter, and 30% use LinkedIn and Facebook.[45]

What Not to Do with Your B2B Email Newsletter

1. Don't include everything. If you have a lot of content, consider breaking it into smaller amounts and sending in multiple deliveries, or headlining items in your newsletter and pushing readers to your website for the full content. Lengthy newsletters can be a turnoff, so keep content as concise as possible.

2. Don't send too frequently. People are trained for newsletters to be a weekly, bi-monthly, or monthly type of broadcast. If you need to send corporate content more often than once a week, you need to make sure that is clear to your recipients when they subscribe.

3. Don't cater to the minority. Are you listening to your feedback? Great! It's important, but make sure you represent the needs of your entire audience and not just the ones who provide feedback.

4. Don't make it all about you. If you offer no value to your readers, they'll get no value from your campaigns. Newsletter content shouldn't be totally self-serving. Offer tips, resources, case studies, research, or other content that will help recipients become more educated, and thereby establish your brand as both helpful and knowledgeable.

5. Don't ignore the recipient. Because email newsletters are about your business, it's easy to fall into the trap of only including content that is very promotional in nature. Remember the 80/20 rule when creating newsletters—80% information, 20% promotion. If you try to balance your content so that it provides more value than promotion, you should end up with a balance that readers can handle.

TAKEAWAY

Don't value your campaign more than you value the recipient.

Winner's Circle
- Have a goal for your email newsletters.
- Create content for all audiences, or segment data and create content for multiple types of recipients.
- Build a content hub and link readers from your email to your website where they can access, search, and share email content. Do not create informative content for an email campaign that can't be found outside of the email.
- Observe the 80/20 rule when creating email content—80% informational and 20% promotional.
- Review your email analytics to use behavioral data to decide on content for future newsletters.
- Do not include too much content in your
- newsletters, and make sure delivery frequency doesn't overwhelm subscribers. You'll know you have a problem if open and click rates drop and unsubscribes increase.
- Do not make your email content self-serving. Provide value to the recipient by including informative content.

PART THREE: The Message: What You Need To Know

CHAPTER 13
Mobile: The New Standard

Starting Line
In this chapter you will learn:
- What has been the recent growth in email usage on mobile devices
- How to create mobile-friendly emails
- How to plan content design and layout for mobile emails
- What responsive design is and whether or not you should use it

It's a mobile world. Email is firmly entrenched in the mobile age. Email users are steadily moving off desktop and webmail software to mobile platforms for accessing and sending email.

In fact, 79% of smartphone owners use their devices to read email, which is a higher percentage than those who use their devices to make phone calls.[46]

Because so many mobile owners are using mobile devices to read email, there's been tremendous growth in mobile email activity. As of December 2014, 48% of mobile email opens occur on a smartphone or tablet device (as high as 51% in December 2013), well ahead of webmail (30%) and desktop (22%).[47] This is a significant change from 2011 when both desktop (58%) and webmail (34%) received more email opens than mobile (8%).

Not only are mobile devices being used to access email, but mobile emails are also influencing purchase behavior. Over one-half of U.S. consumers who made at least one purchase using a smartphone did so because of an email accessed on a mobile device.[48]

Another study found that nearly 75% of consumers are "highly likely" to delete an email immediately if it doesn't display correctly in their mobile inbox.[49] They don't save it for later or temporarily ignore it—it's deleted on the spot.

PART THREE: The Message: What You Need To Know

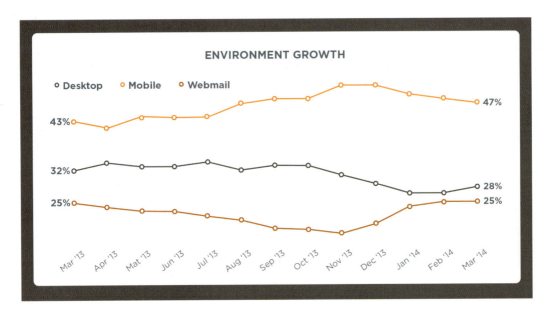

56% say email leads to purchase – more than any other marketing channel.⁵⁰

This activity isn't restricted to younger recipients either. Fully 66% of consumers over age 60 open emails on a mobile device.⁵¹ So with all the impact that mobile has on email marketing, you might think that marketers would be rushing to make their email messaging mobile friendly. But that evolution has been slow to take shape. In fact, 71% of companies and 67% of agencies have said they have basic or no email optimization strategy for mobile devices.⁵²

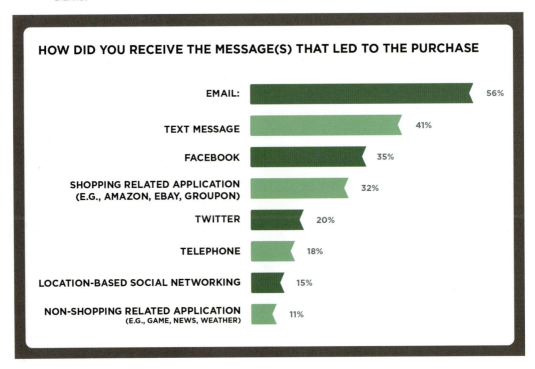

This lack of attention to mobile email optimization is affecting the success rate of email campaigns. Even though nearly half of all recipients are opening emails on mobile devices, the number of recipients clicking on an email is only 11%, which is half the rate of desktop emails (23%).[53]

Many marketers are missing a big opportunity by not planning and executing mobile-friendly email campaigns. Marketers need to implement mobile-first strategies that rely on optimizing email messaging content, design, and calls to action. Without it, campaign effectiveness will suffer dramatically.

How to Create Mobile-Friendly Emails

A mobile-optimized email will provide a positive viewing experience in all environments: desktop, webmail, tablet, and smartphone. Marketers who take the time to optimize their emails across all devices and platforms not only will provide a better user experience, but also will be rewarded with activity and conversions from all recipients. Additionally, there will be less negative brand association, which will help marketers across all channels.

In order to create a mobile-friendly email, marketers will need to make adjustments from the traditional desktop preparation mentality. Many changes will require subtle shifts in approach, but others may require a full redesign and additional programming expertise.

The good news is there are plenty of ways to gain expertise in preparing mobile email campaigns. A few searches will reveal plenty of mobile email marketing blog posts, white papers, e-books, webinars, and more. You can also find free mobile-optimized email templates that you can download and modify. But if you don't have the time to research and prepare mobile emails internally, hiring an agency or other talent will likely be a good investment as the results of a mobile-optimized campaign will likely yield improvements in campaign results, which will likely cover the cost of the outsourced assistance.

In order to prepare mobile-friendly emails, here's a run-down of all the various elements and tips for how they should be optimized for a mobile email environment.

PART THREE: The Message: What You Need To Know

From Name

The from name is the first thing people see in their inbox. If someone doesn't recognize the brand name or person sending the email, it has a much higher chance of being deleted. Be sure to use an easily recognized business name or person name as the from name.

Most Apple devices display a maximum of 23 characters in the from name line (in traditional portrait orientation), so your from name should be short and concise. Anything beyond 23 characters will be cut off. Most Android, Windows, and Blackberry smartphones have similar character limitations, although most tablet devices will typically display about 50 to 70 characters in the from name line.

TIP
Winning tactic: use 23 characters or fewer in your from name.

Subject Lines

Preparing subject lines can be difficult even without restrictions, and being limited to character counts by mobile displays makes it even more of a challenge.

The iPhone 5 and iPad will display 38 or 39 characters in the subject line, but some Android smartphones will only display 33 characters (Galaxy 4s) or 34 characters (Galaxy Note II). However, tablet devices will display up to 84 (Galaxy Nexus, Nexus 7 and Kindle Fire 8.9").[54]

TIP
Winning tactic: front load subject lines. Deliver your offer or message in the first 38 characters or less.

Always front load your subject. This way, even if it gets cut off in an inbox or mobile display, the recipient will still understand the message content or offer.

Preheaders

In the mobile inbox, email preheaders will play an even more important role for marketers as they appear with the from name and subject line in the recipient's initial email display. This is true for Apple and Android platforms. However, you only have a limited space to provide that additional marketing message.

TIP
Winning tactic: Consider the preheader as a way to support the subject line. Use 80 characters or less.

A preheader should be used to support the subject line with an additional message. And on mobile displays, 80 characters or fewer will ensure it is fully displayed in the mobile inbox.

Content Considerations

Displaying an email on a mobile device quickly exposes areas for improvement. You'll see if your message is too lengthy or if your call-to-action isn't in a proper location. Your content hierarchy is also important; you need to immediately capture attention and then provide an easy way for recipients to browse through your content and dig into what matches their interests.

So how should you approach your email content considering a large portion of recipients could be reading it on a smartphone or tablet? Keep these winning tactics in mind.

1. Keep content short and to the point. Remember that people will skim your email, find the content or offer that interests them, and then decide how they want to take action. Shorter, skimmable content works best for mobile users.

2. Make it easy to click. Your call to action, whether a link or a button, should be in a prominent placement and should be easy to click. The clickable area should stand apart from other clickable options so that recipients can easily use their fingers to click your button or link.

You may want to consider having your call to action both at the top of the message and at the bottom. Interested recipients can go right to your site, and others who may want to read and understand more can browse the rest of the email and then click through when finished (without having to scroll back to the top).

87% of clicks will happen when a reader opens an email for the first time. One out of every three clicks occurs on a mobile device.[55]

3. Use content sections and stack them. Many interface elements will span the width of the smartphone display and stack multiple items on top of each other. This creates stacked blocks of content that users can scroll through by moving the screen in an up/down fashion. Your mobile email should take this same approach. Mobile users are already used to this kind of content display and find it intuitive to navigate.

Also prioritize your content, so the most-important information is at the top of the message, and the lesser-important underneath.

4. Remove, nest, or link to low-priority content. Because you have less display area on mobile platforms than on traditional desktop displays, you may need to reconsider how you handle your lower-priority content. You may want to provide a link to

PART THREE: The Message: What You Need To Know

it on your mobile-friendly website, you may want to nest it using responsive design (more on this later), or you may want to remove it entirely. Consider how important it really is and whether you want it to distract from the potential of someone clicking through on your main call-to-action.

Design and Layout

After years of preparing emails for desktop clients, many marketers find it hard to prepare messaging for smaller-format displays. It requires rethinking your content, technical approach, and design.

But with a few small changes marketers can create great-looking, mobile-friendly emails. And it's not terribly difficult to take it a step beyond and create multiple versions of each campaign, so the correct one displays depending on which device a user views the email.

Here are a few pointers to design more mobile-friendly email.

1. Simplify layouts. Review your emails and try to reduce your content only to whatever is necessary to reach your business goals. Consider each element and remove whatever is unnecessary.

2. Plan for iOS scaling. The Apple devices will scale your email to a smaller size, so it displays within an iPhone or iPad environment. Design your email so that it looks good even at a smaller size, and make sure your main content or offer is clear. Also consider how your call-to-action buttons look and work when displayed in the scaled-down version. Make things readable and clickable at the scaled-down size.

3. Use stacks, not columns. If you're still using email templates with a sidebar or multiple columns, chances are you're wreaking havoc for your mobile readers. When an email gets scaled down, it can make columns even smaller and create extra-long pillars of content that require constant scrolling in order to read.

Instead, create content in blocks and stack them on top of each other. Use the full width of the screen. This makes it easier for readers to scan and read your message.

4. Design for touch. Smartphone recipients will use their fingers to scroll and click on your message links and buttons. Make it easy for them.

- Buttons should be 44 x 44 pixels minimum with 10 pixel padding to accommodate touch.
- Design entire sections to be clickable.
- Consider adding clickable space around buttons.
- Create longer text links as they provide more room for touch.
- Do not use small navigation or menu bars or social media icons.

5. Make it readable. It seems counter-intuitive to make things bigger for your mobile displays, but that's actually what is required in order for things to display well on a smaller-format device. Proper mobile design will have fonts and buttons that are generally larger than what most designers use to prepare for desktop recipients.

- Use clean, clear fonts.
- Headline fonts should be at least 30 pixels.
- Body copy fonts should be at least 14 pixels.
- Avoid using fonts below 13 pixels.

iOS will auto-scale small text sizes up to 13 pixels. This may break your layout. This can be overwritten using code. iOS devices will change dates, times, and addresses to clickable blue links. You can use styles to override those changes.

6. Use images carefully. One of the nice things that has happened with the rise of the iOS platforms is that they auto-load images by default, reducing the fear of using imagery in your email messaging. It's still a safe bet to use text to deliver your main offer and use images to supplement your text content, but if you know your audience is mostly using iOS devices or clients that don't have images off by default, then using more imagery can be an option.

When using images, remember to generate simple, bold imagery that looks good even when scaled down, and always reduce images to their file-size minimum, so they load quickly even for mobile users who may be on low-bandwidth data networks.

Responsive Design

Responsive design uses one HTML file that includes CSS and media queries to display certain content and layout based on the device displaying the email. You can use responsive design to create a customized mobile email experience.

PART THREE: The Message: What You Need To Know

You've probably experienced this in your inbox. You may see an email that looks one way in your desktop email client and another way in your mobile inbox. Here's an example of how a responsive email displays in both environments.

Desktop Display

Mobile Display

Responsive Design Benefits:
- It creates a truly mobile optimized message.
- Allows content to be re-formatted specifically for mobile users.
- Allows content to be hidden or revealed for mobile versus desktop users.

Responsive Design Options:
- Change font sizes for better legibility.
- Hide, move, or wrap blocks of content.
- Resize an image.
- Hide or move an image.
- Swap, crop, or hide a background image.

Responsive Design Challenges:
- It doesn't display consistently across all email platforms.
- It requires designing at least two versions of the message.
- Programming can be complicated.
- It requires additional testing and quality control.

STAT — 11.9% of emails with responsive design are clicked compared with 9.8% of non-responsive emails—a 2% click-to-open increase.[56]

Responsive design is slowly becoming a standard and is being implemented by many top brands. Is responsive design right for you?

First understand how many mobile recipients you have in your audience. Then check how your email looks in a mobile display (both Android and iOS). If you notice that you have a significant number of mobile recipients or if your email is not effective on a mobile device, then you may want to test using responsive design for your email campaign. Using responsive design has shown to result in a lift in click-through rates as it makes browsing and acting on an email easier for the user.

PART THREE: The Message: What You Need To Know

Winner's Circle

- Nearly half of all emails are opened on mobile devices. Prepare your emails so they work in a mobile environment.
- Adjust your email content for mobile. Keep content short, use content sections, remove or link to low-priority content, and make calls-to-action easy to click.
- To design your emails for mobile, simplify your layouts, plan for scaling, stack your content (no columns), and design for touch.
- Consider using responsive design to create a customized mobile email experience.

CHAPTER 14
Beyond the Email

Starting Line

In this chapter you will learn:
- What to consider when creating landing pages
- What to consider when conducting surveys
- How to integrate social media into your email campaigns
- Why you should consider including videos in your email campaigns

Winning Tactics for Landing Pages

When planning your email campaign, always plan and test what happens after the click. A great email can be ruined by a lackluster post-click experience. Whether you send recipients to your website, a landing page, a survey, a social media site, or any other destination, you must ensure that your destination is a natural progression from your email campaign and that there is a clear goal to achieve the results you desire.

With that in mind, here are some winning tactics for the landing page or other post-click experience.

Winning Landing Page Tactic #1: Make it a seamless experience.

When an email recipient clicks from your email to your landing page, the message and visual experience should feel like a progression. The message or offer from your email should be supported on a landing page, and the look and feel of the landing page should be similar to the email.

Winning Landing Page Tactic #2: Create an obvious path.

When a user takes action on your email message, they are interested in your content or offer. When they get to your landing page, make it obvious what they need to do to convert. If you want them to fill out a form, download content, or make a purchase, make it easy for them to do so.

PART THREE: The Message: What You Need To Know

Winning Landing Page Tactic #3:
Keep important content above the fold.

Make sure users can easily find the most important content and that everything necessary to complete the conversion exists above the fold. Users should not have to scroll to take action.

Winning Landing Page Tactic #4:
Make it mobile friendly.

A significant number of your recipients will check their email on their mobile devices, so make sure your email and website are optimized for mobile. If a user follows through on your email message from a smartphone or tablet, the web experience should not create technical challenges. Make sure the goals of your campaign can be achieved no matter the user's platform, whether it's desktop, mobile, or a combination of the two. Test to ensure everything works in all environments.

Winning Landing Page Tactic #5:
Don't leave them stranded.

If you bring a user to a landing page and they want to learn more about your business before taking action on your offer, be sure to give them a way to do so. Provide links to your home page, social channels and other relevant content. That way, they can do their due diligence and then follow through on your offer.

Winning Tactics for Surveys

Winning Survey Tactic #1:
Have a goal.

If you want to conduct a survey, you must have a reason for doing so. Are you questioning something about your product or business? Are you confirming or disproving something? Is there something you need to learn that you can't find out any other way?

Whatever your reason, make sure you have a goal. Confirm that you can't get the data you need through other business channels before you ask your contacts to take time from their day to give you the information you desire. Then set up the survey so that the responses will provide the data you need to fulfill the survey goal.

Winning Survey Tactic #2: Provide incentive.

You are asking someone to give up their time and knowledge to provide you with information you need. Give something back in return. At minimum, provide survey takers with the results when the survey is complete.

If that's information that should be kept private, then reward them with some other incentive: a coupon, a gift card, a chance to win a prize, a free white paper, free research, or something else that will provide incentive to those you want to take the survey.

If possible, reward the users immediately after survey completion on the thank-you page or via email. If that's not possible, let the user know when the incentives will be rewarded.

Winning Survey Tactic #3: State the survey length.

If you want someone to give up their time to take your survey, let them know in advance how much time it will take. That way, they can jump right in or save it for when they have more time available. If your survey has a set number of questions, state that up front. If the question length varies depending on answers provided, estimate the survey length and state that when asking for people to respond.

Winning Survey Tactic #4: Keep it short and simple.

The shorter the survey, the more likely you are to get people to take it, and the more likely you are to get people to complete it. Your survey should keep the number of questions to the bare minimum you need to gather quality data, and the answers should be easy to choose and select. Complex charts and rating scales will likely turn off your recipients and possibly lead to unfinished surveys.

This survey from a major financial institution offers too many choices:

PART THREE: The Message: What You Need To Know

What was the main reason for your call to the [bank name] Customer Service Center?
- ○ Incorrect deposit or check amount posted to my account
- ○ Dispute transaction
- ○ Discuss deposit / check / payment held / did not post
- ○ Online banking issue / problem / access issues
- ○ Inquire about / dispute fees
- ○ Replace lost or stolen ATM / debit / credit card
- ○ Request new / additional / replacement ATM / debit / credit card
- ○ Report account fraud / suspicious activity / file claim
- ○ Check balance on account
- ○ See if a check / debit / purchase cleared
- ○ Transfer funds between accounts
- ○ Open an account
- ○ Close an account
- ○ Issue stop payment
- ○ Change information on account (address, phone, add a person to account)
- ○ Inquire about hold on account / card
- ○ Order checks / check status of a check delivery
- ○ Get a copy of a check or statement / combine statements / change statement delivery type (paper / electronic)
- ○ Obtain routing number
- ○ Notify about vacation plans / going out of country
- ○ Notify about large / unusual purchase
- ○ Wire transfer / Safe Send / send money to Mexico / Internationally
- ○ Overdraft protection (linking accounts) – enroll, change or ask questions
- ○ Activate my new or reissued card
- ○ Balance transfer / obtain cash
- ○ Disputing a charge
- ○ Interest rate inquiry
- ○ Update information on my account
- ○ Balance inquiry
- ○ Review individual charges
- ○ Inquiry about points rewards
- ○ Replace a card / add user
- ○ Late fee inquiry
- ○ Inquiry about a payment due date
- ○ Inquiry about my finance charges
- ○ Make a payment / find out about payment options
- ○ Credit line inquiry
- ○ Report a lost or stolen card
- ○ Close my account
- ○ Annual fee inquiry
- ○ Online access / issues
- ○ Stop receiving convenience checks in th email
- ○ Fraud alert email / report fraud / phishing

Winning Survey Tactic #5: Write quality questions and answers.

Keep your questions and answers clear and to the point. Ask about one thing at a time and make sure you cover all possible answers without overlapping. Don't violate your survey's integrity by writing loaded, biased, or misleading questions. And make sure you don't steer any of your questions towards a particular answer.
Examples:
Bad: How do you like our redesigned emails?
Better: How do you feel about our redesigned emails?
Bad: We have redesigned our website to become an industry-leading destination. What do you think of our site improvements?
Better: What are your thoughts on our redesigned website?

Winning Survey Tactic #6: Use The Data You Gather.

If you are taking the time and effort to gather data, then use the data you collect to make an improvement to your business. All survey results should be analyzed with an eye toward using that data to make an actionable change.

Winning Tactics for Social Media

Many businesses include social media options in their email marketing. These social media links tend to fall into one of three categories:

1. Links to share email content via a social channel
2. Links to a brand's social channel home page
3. Links directly to social channel content

The first two are the most common—many B2B emails include ways to share email content, and many brands will include links to their social channels (which are now generally found in the email header or footer areas). The goal of sharing email content is to provide ways for recipients to spread your message and provide additional exposure. The goal of including links to social channels is to gain additional followers.

If you are linking directly to social content, the goal is to encourage participation in a social post or thread. You want to encourage feedback and increase engagement. Marketers can do this by highlighting the social post and asking for recipients to participate.

PART THREE: The Message: What You Need To Know

Make it easy for them to provide feedback, answer a question, or participate in whatever way is most appropriate.

When brands want to provide social sharing in their emails, they should consider these tactics:

Winning Social Media Tactic #1:
Keep the sharing options near the content.

It should be clear to recipients that they are able to share the content they are enjoying, and the icons or links should be placed near the sharable content. Make icon placement obvious and intuitive.

Winning Social Media Tactic #2:
Make icons easy to click, even on mobile.

It's common for marketers to want to include the social sharing icons in bunches, which makes it difficult for users to click, especially when using their thumbs on mobile devices. Make sure to spread icons out and pad them so that the icons are clickable, even when scaled down on a mobile display.

Here's an example showing social sharing icons with proper placement and padding:

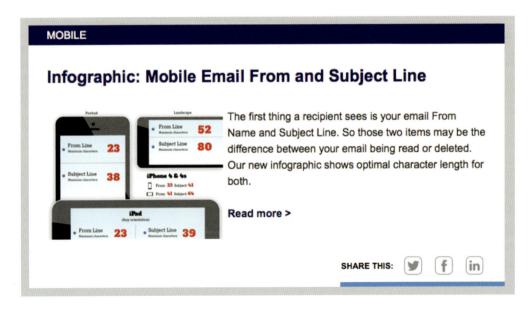

Winning Social Media Tactic #3: Remove unnecessary icons.

Many marketers will include all kinds of social icons, even if their audience doesn't use most of them. Marketers will likely find that LinkedIn, Twitter, and Facebook will be the most-accessed sharing icons. If you include other icons beyond those, watch your click metrics to ensure they're being used. If not, remove them.

Winning Tips for Video

Partnering video with email is one of the sure-fire ways to draw additional interest to your email and to your video content. Statistics show that people prefer to watch video in place of reading text. So if you want to bump up your email marketing opens, click-through and conversion rates, consider incorporating video.

Simply including the word "video" in an email's subject line saw an increase of 7 to 13% in overall click-through rates (CTRs), and embedding a video in an email generated an average conversion rate 21% higher than emails containing a static image alone.[57] And in a study of 800,000 emails, those containing video received, on average, 5.6% higher open rates and 96.4% higher CTRs than non-video emails.[58]

There are several ways to use video in your email marketing. The most common tactics include:

Winning Video Tactic #1: Video thumbnail.

This approach is the most common. Marketers embed a static image that represents a video. Upon click, the user is taken to a web-hosted video.

Winning Video Tactic #2: Embedded video.

This tactic is less common but gaining popularity. Although video is still not something that can be embedded in emails across all platforms and clients, there are some scenarios that allow for embedded video.

Winning Video Tactic #3: Animated GIF.

Using a .gif file to replicate a video experience is a safe option as long as the recipient can support the bandwidth required for the image animation.

PART THREE: The Message: What You Need To Know

Best practices for including video in your email include:

1. Mention "Video" in the subject line.

2. Place the video in a prominent location so those coming to watch the video can do so immediately.

3. Include a PLAY button in the video player or player image, so it's clear that the user will gain access to video content.

4. Keep videos as short as possible. Many viewers lose interest after a few minutes.

5. Display the length of video. Short videos will likely attract immediate clicks, while longer videos may be saved and returned for viewing later.

6. Include an additional call to action or link in your email just in case the video embed or video image doesn't load or display properly.

7. Provide a path for the user AFTER the video has played. Give them a way to take action on the video message.

8. Remember that creating video has many benefits beyond email, including additional value for search and increased stickiness on websites.

If you are considering adding video to your email campaigns, don't be afraid to give it a test. It's proven to be a successful tactic for anyone willing to put forth the effort to develop quality video content. Video can definitely help your brand stand out from the competition and generate more interest from your recipients.

Winner's Circle

- Create landing pages that are mobile friendly and a seamless experience from the email. Make sure the path to conversion is obvious.
- Always have a goal for your surveys. Keep them as short as possible. Only ask for the data you need to achieve your goal.
- Keep social sharing icons near their content, and only include sharing for channels that your readers use. Remove icons if users aren't sharing with them.
- Test using video in your emails, even if it's a thumbnail that links to a video or a video-like animated GIF. Also mention it in the subject line. Watch opens and clicks increase.

PART FOUR:
Know Your Audience:
Deliver Relevance

CHAPTER 15
Segmentation and Personalization

Starting Line
In this chapter you will learn:
- What the difference is between personalization and segmentation
- Why increasing relevance will increase results
- Why personalization increases open, click-through and conversion rates
- What list segmentation strategies to employ
- How to segment with marketing personas

Recipients want to receive emails that they find interesting and relevant. They want the email to speak directly to their interests. The problem is, not all recipients are the same. They have different problems, different responsibilities, and different challenges. **There is no one-size-fits-all solution to email marketing.**

STAT **Relevant emails drive 18 times more revenue than broadcast emails.**[59]

As email marketing progresses, delivery of relevant communications is becoming more crucial to a program's success. Studies show that irrelevant messaging is the top reason for recipients unsubscribing from a campaign. So how do marketers create more relevant emails? How do you deliver messaging that speaks directly to the recipient? *You do this through segmentation and personalization.*

Personalization is the process of crafting messages to an individual's preferences or interests.

Segmentation is the process of defining and subdividing a large set of data into smaller portions based on similarities in data, actions, or interests.

Personalization

Email marketing that is personalized to the recipient will almost always result in better response. A whopping 96% of organizations

TAKEAWAY

If you aren't slicing and dicing your email database into various segments, tailoring your content to those groups of recipients, you're reducing the value of your message and minimizing your potential to reach your goals.

TIP

Increasing email relevance on an individual level will always generate better results. Relevance = Results.

believe that email personalization can improve email marketing performance.[60] Personalized emails improve open rates by 26%,[61] click-through rates by 14%, and conversion rates by 10%.[62]

Despite the benefits of personalization, 68% of marketers aren't utilizing personalization techniques in their campaigns.[63] With 72% of B2B firms reporting that "delivering highly relevant content" is a top priority, it seems that B2B marketers who employ personalization techniques will easily stand out from their competition.

Email Personalization Options

The ability to personalize email messages comes from having data on your contacts. If you have any personal information, professional information, previous activity, or other data, you can likely use that to your advantage in your email.

Here are some ways to personalize your email campaigns:

1. Subject line. Although the trend of including a recipient's name in the subject line has largely died off due to overuse, including other types of data in your subject lines may prove the difference between getting opened or deleted.

Use data to your advantage. Try personalizing subject lines with data that will speak directly to the recipient. Here are some examples for using job titles, geographic data, and user history:

- *Free e-book download for* **marketing directors**
- *Your* **New York** *customers will appreciate our new insurance policy*
- *If you* **liked widget A,** *don't miss the new widget B!*

2. Message body copy. Using data to personalize the content in your message can prove very effective. If you start a message with several personalized data points, the recipient will likely become engaged and take interest in the rest of your content.

A good example of using personalized data in message content:

Hi, [first name]. We enjoyed meeting you at [event name]. We just released several new white papers that may help you with your marketing efforts at [your company].

3. Images. Images can be a powerful part of your email message, but one image may not provide the same impact to your entire audience. Consider swapping out images based on job role, gender, geography, or any other data that can help you deliver a more relevant photo, graph, or other visual. Test to see which images resonate best with your recipients.

4. Design & layout. Data can be used to help you determine the most effective design and layout to use for your email. If you know the gender of your recipient, you can use different colors to personalize the message design. Men tend to prefer darker, stronger colors, while women prefer emails with softer, lighter visuals.

5. Content. You can personalize the content of an entire message based on the previous activity or behavior of the recipient. Emails that include recommendations use this technique. Pulling previous purchases, previous interests, survey results, or other data can allow you to create content for each data point and serve up appropriate content into the message.

For example, this email from Twitter displays recommended accounts to follow based on your previous follow activity.

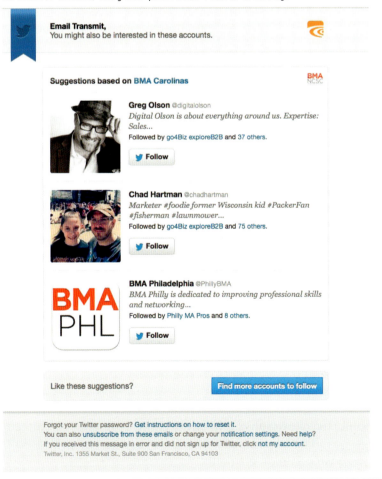

6. Content ordering. If you know the job role of your recipient, you may want to re-order the content of your messages differently for those in the C-suite or other senior positions. You'll want decision makers to see the content that captures their attention prior to any other content targeted at other positions, such as "how-to" articles or checklists.

Personalization is not just limited to one message—it can also go beyond a single email to creating entire campaigns. Take personalization to the next level by using automation, where emails are automatically sent to a recipient based on their action or non-action.

Segmentation

Strategic Tactics for Segmentation

Delivering the right message at the right time to the right audience has always been at the core of email marketing success. And according to a 2013 *BtoB Magazine* survey, marketers see "delivering content relevant to a segment" as the most important tactic to improving email marketing performance.[64] Nearly half of all marketers feel this tactic will help them improve their email marketing results.

Along with this, list segmentation was also recognized by 30% of B2B marketers as a tactic to improve marketing performance.[65] And Marketo's "Benchmark on Email Marketing" survey found segmentation to be the highest ROI tactic used by email marketers, higher than drip marketing or dynamic content.[66]

By combining list segmentation and segment-specific content, marketers could see a dramatic increase in the quality and performance of their campaigns. So why aren't more marketers implementing segmentation strategies?

List Segmentation Strategies

The four basic segmentation strategies are based on behavioral, demographic, psychographic, and geographical differences.

Behavioral segmentation should be central to your segmentation strategy. Recipients can be broken into groups by engagement metrics.

Demographic, psychographic, and geographic segments can be determined based on commonalities, and content can be produced to speak to those common elements.

How To Win At B2B Email Marketing

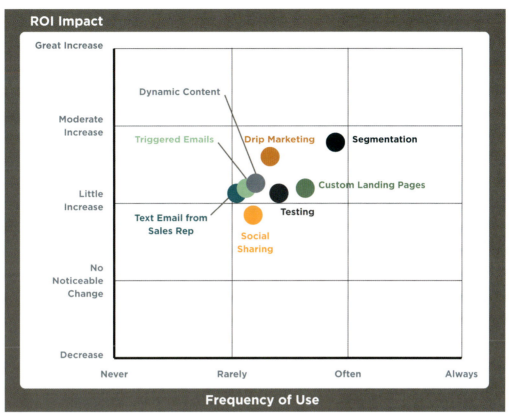

Breaking apart your database into segments based on gender, interests, or region, and writing content specifically for those segments can lend to highly personalized campaigns and quality results.

Segmentation is used often by marketers as it results in an increase in ROI impact.[67]

Segmentation Options

1. Market segment. Segment by market or product, customer type, or user group. For B2B marketers, this may be one of the best segmentation strategies. If you can speak to your business contacts on a market-by-market level, you'll likely be providing highly relevant, useful content.

2. Behavior. Those who frequently open messages, click on links, and generate conversions are likely to be the most valuable contacts in your marketing database. Treat those records with utmost care and give them the attention they deserve. You may even want to consider special programs or special offers specifically for this segment.

Those showing little or no activity might be segmented out for a re-engagement campaign. Surveys, contests, sweepstakes, special offers, and polls may provide enough interest to re-awaken these connections and spark an increase in engagement.

3. Demographics. Segment by age, gender, or other demographic information you have on your business contacts. You may communicate to a young professional differently than a worker nearing retirement.

4. Psychographics. Psychographics is the study of values, interests, attitudes, and lifestyles. Collect and use psychographic data to your advantage. For example, a B2B product manufacturer may be able to segment on whether its product's price, benefits, safety, or support is most important to its recipients.

5. Geography. Geography is a pretty easy segment to employ. Breaking down recipients by zip code, state, region, or country can help marketers provide a more relevant message.

Are you selling a seasonal product? No need to send your snow-blower-parts discount email to resellers in Florida.

Offering overnight shipping? Remove your international contacts from the campaign.

Are sales lower in a particular region? Break them out for a special offer.

6. Sales cycle stage. Set up separate messages for those at different stages in the sales cycle. If you change your communication approach to those in the early stages of brand awareness versus those who have a long-standing history with your brand, you'll likely produce more effective messages.

7. VICs and lurkers. VICs (very important customers) deserve recognition. They don't want to be treated like everyone else, nor should they be. So find them, separate them, and send them personalized emails that acknowledge their past purchase or contributions.

Also segment your lurkers. They get your emails, but they don't ever respond. Consider sending a message to re-engage them or remind them that there's a special offer or time-sensitive promotion they can access if they take action immediately.

8. User history. Your email database likely contains a lot of actionable, targetable subscriber data accumulated during the history of the relationship. For example, the opt-in date can be used for segmentation. Don't send a new customer the same email that you're sending someone who has been on your email list for 10 years. Or segment by how many emails someone has received or how many they have opened.

9. Job role, title, or position. Although this can be difficult due to the lack of standard in job role titles, it may be useful to target various contacts at businesses by job role. Segmenting by C-level employees, directors, or other positions allows you to prepare messaging using the language and content that would speak to someone at that position.

10. Size of business. It's no secret that small businesses operations vary drastically from large businesses. Small businesses may be faster to move due to fewer processes and people involved in the decision-making process. If you sell or connect to contacts at businesses that range in size, you may want to segment your database by business size to deliver appropriate messaging to each.

11. Acquired data. You may be sitting on more segmentation data than you think. Data collected via surveys, opt-in forms, preference centers, or expressed interests (via email clicks or website visits) can all be used for segmentation. If you've collected additional data through user opt-in forms, or have conducted surveys, then you likely have a lot of powerful information to help you segment.

The problem many marketers face is with "siloed" data, which comes from other channels, such as social media or point of sale. It's important to bring as much user information into your email marketing mix as possible, so that may mean finding a way to integrate different data elements into the email platform for better targeting.

12. Lead source or subscription method. Where did the lead come from? A trade show? Website opt-in? Download form? Segmenting by the source acquisition point provides a natural way to connect with your audience.

If a lead came from a trade show, for example, prepare a message with a recap of the trade show, how your brand supports the trade show audience, and links to your trade show marketing materials and presentations. This will help you stand out from the mass of brands that an attendee experienced during their time at the trade show.

13. Customer value. Segment by influencers, customer lifetime value (CLV), or other indicators of customer value. Similar to user history, this allows you to speak to users according to their interest in your product or service and their corresponding value as a customer.

14. The leftovers. Don't forget to create your email message to address those you can't segment. These leftover contacts may need a message with broader content and wider appeal. If possible, include polls or surveys, so you can learn more about this group, and provide an incentive for these contacts to round out their profiles.

CASE STUDY

UsedCardboardBoxes.com: B2B Email Alerts Lead to Big ROI.

UsedCardboardBoxes.com (UCB) sells just that: used cardboard boxes. Its business challenge is to purchase used boxes only in the sizes buyers need. Buyers typically buy in bulk, which can result in large orders.

When UCB wants to anticipate demand, it will send a very basic alert email to customers prior to purchasing the inventory. That way they can gauge interest before acquiring the used boxes. The alert email will only go to its segment of customers within a defined geographical area who have either previously purchased or expressed interest in that specific type of cardboard box. UCB then uses responses to gauge how aggressively to bid on the inventory.

The email is very basic, mostly a text message with one image, SKU information, a short description, and a link for a price quote.

The results of the campaign are very effective. A single alert email can generate more than $13,000 in sales.[68] With an average order around $5,000, if an inventory alert generates one order, then it more than covers the cost of the campaign.

This case study was originally prepared by MarketingSherpa. This version has been edited. View the entire case study at http://b2bemailmarketingbook.com/resources.

Segment with Marketing Personas

Creating marketing personas can provide businesses with a way to humanize their marketing audiences. Businesses can create several fictitious people to represent different segments of their audiences, and author content to address those personas.

Creating personas will not only help you identify the similarities and differences of your contacts, but also help you easily "speak" to each. Internally it'll help marketers refer to their various audience segments and will also assist with developing ideas for new marketing content.

To create marketing personas, start by asking the following questions:

1. Who are your typical audiences?
2. What are their key business motivators?
3. What are their biggest challenges?
4. Are they decision makers, or does someone else influence their decisions?
5. What are their common demographics, psychographics, and behaviors?
6. How do they access decision-making information?

Once you've answered the questions, you'll likely notice several groups of people with common characteristics. Each of these common types can now be given a name, which will become your marketing persona.

As you create new content, you can target a particular persona and address its specific needs. Some content may be usable across multiple personas, and other content will address a very particular need of one persona.

Once you have persona-specific content, segment your database for each persona. Then deliver the targeted, relevant messaging you've generated to create a truly valuable experience.

Winner's Circle

- Increasing email relevance on an individual level will always generate better results. **Relevance = Results.**
- **Personalization** is the process of crafting messages to an individual's preferences or interests. **Segmentation** is the process of defining and subdividing a large set of data into smaller portions based on similarities in data, actions, or interests.
- Personalization in emails can occur not only in the subject line but also in message copy, images, design, and layout, and through the ordering of content.
- Delivering content relevant to a segment is the most important tactic to improving email marketing performance.[69]
- Segmentation can occur through the use of behavioral, demographic, psychographic, or geographic data.
- Consider using marketing personas to humanize your marketing audience.

PART FOUR: Know Your Audience: Deliver Relevance

CHAPTER 16
Lead Nurturing and the B2B Sales Cycle

Starting Line

In this chapter you will learn:
- What is lead nurturing and why you should use it
- What role email plays in lead nurturing
- How to nurture leads throughout the B2B sales cycle
- How to customize lead nurturing email content
- What common lead nurturing challenges to watch for along with appropriate solutions

What Is Lead Nurturing?

Lead nurturing guides a prospect through a process of having minimal knowledge about a product or service to being someone who is prepared to become a customer. Research has shown that 73% of B2B leads are still in the early phases of their research and are not ready to make a purchasing decision.[70] Those leads are not ready to engage with sales. For many businesses, it may take weeks to months (or even years) to nurture a lead from being an initial prospect to being sales-ready.

A very small portion of acquired leads will be ready to go directly to the sales team. A small percentage will be bad leads and should be removed from your lead database. The remainder will likely end up purchasing from you or your competition, but are not ready to do so yet. Those are the leads that you want to nurture so that they decide to purchase from your company when buying time arrives.

Why Use Lead Nurturing?

Today's buyers tend to make their way though the initial phases of the buying cycle without intervention from brands. In many cases, buyers will completely research a potential purchase on their own and won't engage with a business until late in the buying cycle. With this in mind, sellers need to provide high-quality content to attract, educate, and assist a buyer to earn their business when they're ready to make a purchase.

PART FOUR: Know Your Audience: Deliver Relevance

Lead nurturing can help businesses:

- Maintain permission to stay in contact with the lead.
- Improve the quality of leads prior to handing them off to sales.
- Create perceived value as a result of trust in the brand or salesperson.
- Shorten a longer sales cycle.

When you execute a successful lead-nurturing program, you can learn more about your lead while gaining an understanding of the prospect's knowledge, interests, and timing. But this will only be possible if you deliver content that's of sufficient value to the right prospect at the right time.

 STAT **Today's business buyers do not contact suppliers directly until 57% of the purchase process is complete.**[71] **This presents a challenge for marketers as they need to be present in multiple channels in order to educate and influence potential purchasing decisions.**

What Role Does Email Play in Lead Nurturing?

Email may be the most important communication channel in the lead-nurturing process. Email marketing can facilitate the lead-nurturing process through a considered stream of relevant, timely, personalized content. Because most lead-nurturing programs will require from five to twenty-five touches to become sales ready, email will likely be the channel in which the majority of those touches take place.

Email not only is used to distribute content, but also can help identify interest levels through the analysis of opens and clicks. For example, if every email sent is being opened and clicked, use that as a trigger to move prospects farther along in the cycle.

Email can also help build and solidify business relationships through the delivery of personalized, highly relevant content. And through the process of delivering valuable content, email will inform and educate contacts, so they are ready to connect with a sales person at the appropriate point in the sales cycle.

Nurturing through the B2B Sales Cycle

Many lead-nurturing programs will require multiple touches to prepare a sales-ready lead. In many cases this is a minimum of five to seven touches, but more likely ten to twenty-five communications will be required. The complexity or expense of your business product or service will largely dictate a typical sales cycle, so understanding how quickly (or slowly) your prospects move through your sales cycle phases will help you understand communication timing and frequency.

Lead nurturing tactics include:

- Segment your leads to deliver the most relevant content to each.
- Analyze what your leads respond to and deliver appropriate content based on their interests.
- Follow up with leads based on their actions.
- Continuously offer valuable content to your audience whether it's self-promotional or not.

Lead nurturing tactics to avoid include:

- Sending the same communication to your entire lead database
- Emailing to "check in" with your lead without offering anything of value.
- Only providing brochure-ware via email.
- Asking for a purchase with every communication.

65% of B2B Marketers have not established lead nurturing campaigns. [72]

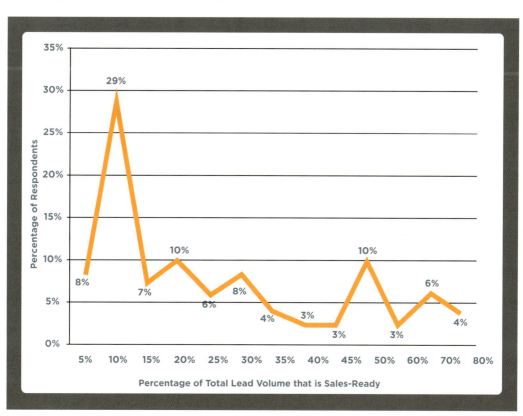

PART FOUR: Know Your Audience: Deliver Relevance

In order to provide value to the leads you are nurturing, you'll need to understand where they are in the sales cycle. Producing content for every stage of the cycle will greatly improve your ability to identify and move buyers from awareness to purchase.

When a marketer looks at a typical buyer's process through the B2B sales cycle, they can map their marketing strategy to the buyer's needs at the various points in the cycle. And by doing so, they can identify what content to deliver, in what channel, and at what sequence.

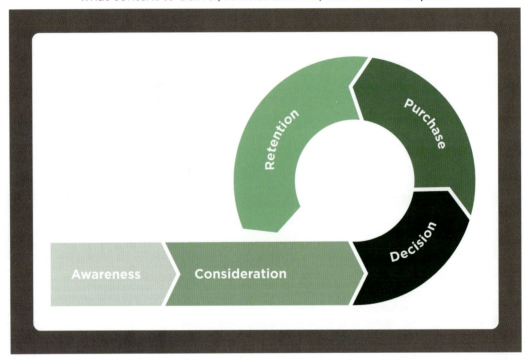

When sellers understand the buyer process, they can effectively plan their marketing approach for each step of the sales cycle. And that approach is key to moving prospects through the cycle more efficiently in order to minimize the time it takes to reach business goals.

1. Awareness. During the awareness stage, leads become aware of a product or service, or they identify a need that must be fulfilled. They commit to making a change. Leads in the awareness stage are beginning to learn about your company and its services and are usually seeking information.

ACTION: When a seller determines that they have a potential buyer in the awareness phase, they will need to acknowledge the buyer, identify the buyer need, and qualify the opportunity. Email can assist with this process in a number of ways. Types of content for those in the awareness stage:

- Welcome email series
- Email newsletters
- White papers
- E-books
- Educational webinars
- Guides
- Checklists
- Cheat sheets
- How-to content
- Informative videos
- Infographics

Sellers must use their email content to help them understand the buyer's needs or requirements. Tracking and analyzing what content sparks interest from the buyer through email opens, clicks, or website activity does that very well. And if sellers enhance that understanding by capturing data through surveys, polls, download forms, and other data collection practices, sellers can better understand the buyer's interests and further qualify the business opportunity.

2. Consideration. During the consideration stage, leads will explore possible solutions to fill their needs. They will evaluate products and services and compare them against competitive options. They will transition from simply being aware a product or service exists to thinking about whether or not an investment in that product or service will help their businesses.

ACTION: When you have potential buyers in this stage, educate them on how your offerings can provide business value. Types of content those in the consideration stage seek:

- Webinars about the product or service
- Data sheets
- Demonstration videos
- FAQs
- Industry research

Throughout the consideration phase, sellers will need to pay close attention to how quickly a potential buyer consumes and digests content. Some buyers will remain in the consideration phase for long periods of time and progress slowly. Others will quickly determine that they will want to make a purchase, and will then move into the next phase of the buying cycle.

PART FOUR: Know Your Audience: Deliver Relevance

Clues that a potential buyer is nearing the end of the consideration phase include an increase in activity around one particular product or service, or moving toward more in-depth content about the item they are interested in pursuing.

3. Decision. In the decision stage, leads have become educated about your products and services and what value they can bring. These leads will complete their research, prioritize their potential solutions, compare them for value, and then go through the necessary internal channels to seek approval for the purchase.

ACTION: Using segmented, personalized campaigns during this phase is a must as the content has to assist the buyer in choosing your product or business for their purchase. Types of content those in the decision stage seek:

- Case studies
- Testimonials
- Comparison information
- Presentations (to share with decision makers)

At this point in the sales cycle the lead is often considered "sales ready." At this time, your sales team should connect with the prospect. A buyer may

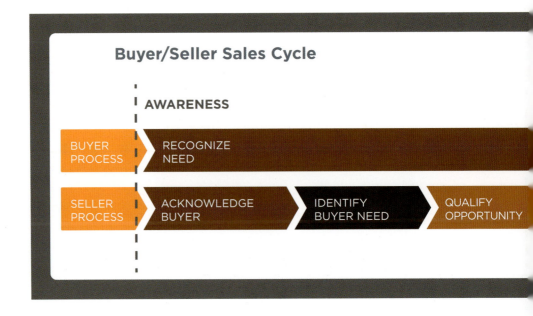

voluntarily connect directly with the seller at this stage. Sellers will need to match the contact with their previous history in order to understand they are nearing a purchase decision.

4. Purchase. At the completion of this stage, all your lead nurturing efforts should be rewarded through a purchase of your product or service. After securing the business, this is a good time to review the path your lead took as they moved through the buying cycle from awareness to purchase. Understanding how a prospect collected information and made decisions and the timing at which it occurred will help you fine-tune your lead nurturing process for future prospects.

ACTION: During this phase, email should be used to provide purchasing incentives to the buyer. The messaging should highlight special offers or options for a buyer to connect with your business. Everything should provide incentive to the buyer to choose your business for their purchase. Types of content those in the purchase stage will seek:

- Free trials
- Live demos
- Consultations
- Proposals or estimates
- Coupons

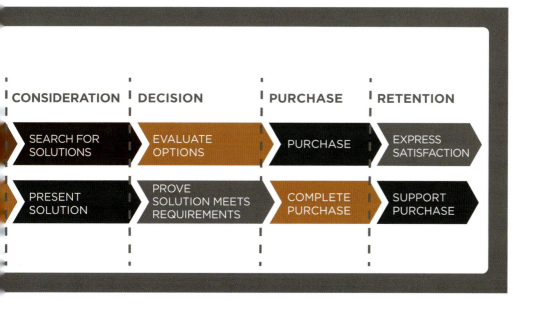

5. Retention. Marketing should not end at the point of a purchase. Your buyers should now move into a retention marketing process, where they are continuously educated.

ACTION: Help buyers maximize their use of your product or service; inform them of complementary products and services they can purchase to enhance their experience. If retention marketing is done well, your buyers not only will continue their business relationship, but also may increase their purchases and become advocates of your brand. Types of content those in the retention stage will seek:

- Product demonstrations
- New product or service announcements
- Webinars on other products and services
- Newsletters
- Educational content

Email should be used throughout the retention phase to deliver content on a regular basis. Customers need to feel appreciated and know they are not forgotten. The more active and engaged they are with your brand, the more chance you have for them to make referrals or recommendations, or even to share their successes through case studies and testimonials.

Customizing Lead Nurturing Email Content

Throughout the lead nurturing process, segmenting and personalizing email content will offer invaluable benefits by providing more relevant information. In order to customize email content, you will need to know not only where a buyer is in the buying cycle but also how other factors will impact their decision making process.

A senior manager at a Fortune 500 company is a much different buyer than an owner of a small business. When messaging speaks to each audience appropriately, you'll have a much better chance of moving them through the sales cycle and ultimately leading them to a purchase. Use dynamic content or prepare different messages for various segments based on data you've collected. Possible data segments that can be used to customize email content include:

- Industry
- Job role
- Decision maker
- Geography
- Company size (small vs. med vs. large biz)
- Product interest

Lead Nurturing Challenges and Solutions

Lead nurturing is a marketing practice that many marketers find intimidating and think is too big a concept for them to execute properly. And while it does generally require some investment and resources, it is not something that should be out of the reach of most organizations. A lead nurturing program can begin with a few pieces of content and the development of a handful of emails and web pages.

But with any objective there comes challenges. And lead nurturing is no exception. Marketers will recognize the following issues with starting or executing a proper lead nurturing program.

Challenge: Not having enough content
Solution: Start small. Develop one piece of content for each segment of the sales cycle, and then continue to develop more topic-specific content down the road.

Challenge: Marketing throughout a long sales cycle
Solution: Lead nurturing shortens the sales cycle. Attempt to connect with prospects more frequently, so you move them toward purchase at a more rapid pace. Develop more content in the parts of the cycle where delays typically occur, and consider human interaction when progress slows.

Challenge: Nurturing leads that are not sales ready
Solution: Keep the touches coming. The only way to progress leads through the sales cycle is to inform and educate. Sending less frequently or ignoring leads that are not showing progress will not lead to them moving forward in the sales cycle. Continue to deliver valuable content, and at some point, the lead will likely move to the next stage.

Challenge: Marketing team hands off unqualified leads too early
Solution: Make sure your leads are demonstrating that they are near the decision stage. Only a small portion of initial leads (usually less than 25%) are sales ready. The rest should be put in the lead nurturing process and only handed off once they are nearing a purchase decision.

Challenge: Sales team takes leads too early and turns off potential buyers
Solution: Any lead that is still asking for introductory-level content is not ready to be handed off to sales. Lead nurturing can help identify

where leads are in the buying cycle and at what point sales should make contact. Avoid making contact too early as that can kill the lead progress and thwart a potential sale.

Challenge: Distributing lead nurturing content
Solution: Many businesses find that marketing automation can simplify the lead nurturing process. Using marketing automation platforms allows businesses to establish rules and ensure that leads receive appropriate content at appropriate times.

Winner's Circle

- The majority of leads are still researching product information and are not ready to be handed off to the sales team. Nurture those leads, so they decide to purchase from your company when they are ready to do so.
- Most lead nurturing programs will require from five to twenty-five touches to become sales ready. Email will likely be the channel in which the majority of those touches take place.
- Producing content for every stage of the cycle will greatly improve your ability to identify and move buyers from awareness to purchase.
- Marketers should map their marketing strategies to buyers' needs at the various points in the sales cycle. By doing so, they can identify what content to deliver, in what channel, and at what sequence.
- Throughout the lead nurturing process, segment and personalize email content to provide a more relevant marketing experience.

How To Win At B2B Email Marketing

CHAPTER 17
Frequency and Cadence

Starting Line

In this chapter you will learn:
- How often you should send marketing emails
- What factors indicate you are sending too much or not enough email

One of the biggest challenges marketers face is how many emails to send to their contacts. If you don't send enough, you risk leaving money on the table. If you send too many, you risk turning off your recipients and increasing numbers of unsubscribes. How many emails should you send? What frequency is not enough? How many emails are too many?

When looking at reasons why people unsubscribe from receiving email campaigns, frequency holds the top spot, having recently overtaken relevance. While that probably isn't a surprise, it shows how important it is for marketers to understand how often they should be communicating with their subscribers.

Frequency continues to be the top reason why people unsubscribe. Relevance is also a key reason. However, brand fatigue is seldom a factor. [73]

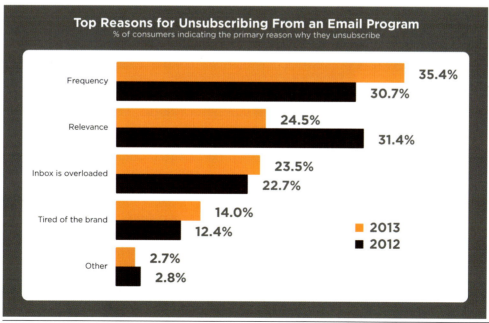

151

PART FOUR: Know Your Audience: Deliver Relevance

TIP

Pay close attention to your reporting. It'll show you where fatigue sets in and your revenue per campaign starts to decline.

When trying to determine an optimal email frequency you should first put yourself in the shoes of the recipient. How often would you want to receive your emails? Are you providing value with every communications? How often do your recipients need your content, products, or services?

Look at the sales cycle. Are you selling something that recipients only purchase once every few years? You probably don't need to be sending emails more often than once or twice a month. Delivering special offers on office supplies that are recurring purchases? Sending emails several times a week may be appropriate.

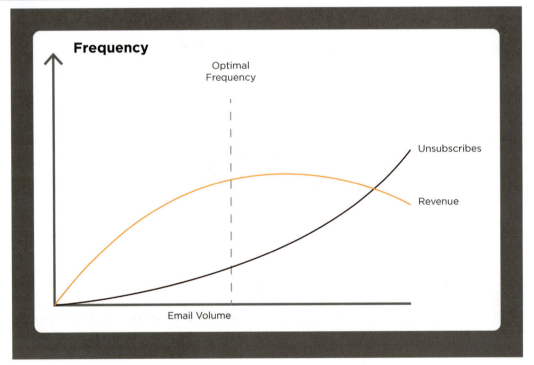

Determining where fatigue sets in may be realized through more than just declines in revenue. Other indicators include:

- Declines in opens
- Declines in click-throughs
- Declines in web page views after email click-through
- Declines in length of web visits after email click-through
- Increase in complaints from subscribers

On the other hand, there are several indicators that you may not be emailing enough. Those include:

- High or inconsistent levels of engagement. If you find some

campaigns do abnormally well, then that may mean your audience is primed for more content or offers.
- High percentages of bounce backs. If you are experiencing lots of bounce backs, then too many contacts are going bad between campaigns.
- Increase of non-email volume to your website (especially return visits). If people are willingly coming to your site and doing so frequently, they probably won't mind hearing from you more often.

Frequency with Targeting

It's typical for a list of subscribers to include active and inactive members. Actives will open and click frequently, while inactives register limited or no responses. Should you be marketing to both the same way? Many marketers are now segmenting their databases and mailing different campaigns to those who actively participate versus those who seldom or never participate. Actives will receive email more often, based on their interests and participation with the brand.

Winner's Circle
- Optimal email frequency occurs at the peak of email-driven revenue but before an upturn in unsubscribes.
- Determining where frequency fatigue sets in can be analyzed through decreases in opens, click-throughs, website page views, and length of visit.
- Email more frequently if you have high levels of engagement, few unsubscribes, and an increase in website visits and traffic.

PART FOUR: Know Your Audience: Deliver Relevance

CHAPTER 18
Automated Campaigns

Starting Line

In this chapter you will learn:
- What the automated campaign benefits are
- What the three automated campaign phases are
- Whether or not to use marketing automation software

Automated campaigns (also sometimes referred to as auto responders) are a follow-up process where prepared email communications are delivered at pre-determined intervals. The messaging can be specific to the call to action from which the lead came, the timing of the acquisition of the lead, or based on user activity.

Automated campaigns tend to be a series of communications that are often sent following an email opt-in or after a particular user action, such as an open, a click-through, a download, attending a webinar, or abandoning a shopping cart. They may also be used based on a non-action, such as a re-engagement campaign or a campaign targeting those who have expressed interest but have not completed a desired action over a certain period of time.

The benefits of automated campaigns include:
1. Reduced manual processes
2. Timely, relevant communications at appropriate times
3. Streamlined lead nurturing process
4. Ensured regular communications to contacts
5. Accessible data on the lead nurturing process
6. Simplified identification of highly engaged leads

Types of automated campaigns can include drip and nurture campaigns. Many businesses do not distinguish between the two, but are likely doing one, the other, or both.

Drip Campaigns

A drip campaign is a series of prepared email communications that will be sent on a predetermined schedule. They are intended for a broad audience—likely anyone who is in the subscriber database.

Drip campaigns can be designed to educate subscribers, define brand positioning, provide marketing offers, or recognize various milestones. They will be sent at different times to different subscribers depending on the event that triggers the drip campaign. Those events may include:

1. Calendar date. A drip campaign may be set to start on a specific date, such as a holiday, birthday, or anniversary.

2. Pre-determined schedule. A drip campaign may be sent based on a schedule X number of days after an opt-in or milestone.

An example of a drip campaign is a *new subscriber welcome series.* A welcome series is delivered to new opt-ins at pre-determined intervals after they subscribe to a list. It is an effective way to position a brand and educate a new subscriber. A new subscriber welcome series may include content such as a thank-you email from the CEO, an email with recent press or industry news, an email that includes product or service benefits, etc.

The responses or actions from a drip campaign may position a subscriber to move into a nurture campaign.

Nurture Campaigns

A nurture campaign is a series of prepared email communications that will be sent to a segmented audience based on an action or each subscriber's place in the buying cycle. They are intended for a specific audience and are crafted to be fine-tuned to speak directly to a small portion of the subscriber database.

There will usually be several nurture campaigns created to address the various segments within a subscriber database. The goal of a nurture campaign is to move subscribers farther along in the sales cycle by educating them on a certain topic. There are several types of nurture campaigns including:

1. Interest—sent to opt-in subscribers after they express interest in a certain type of content, such as visiting various parts of your website multiple times;

2. Milestone—triggered when a recipient reaches a trackable milestone such as number of purchases made or length of time as a customer; and

3. Transactional—delivered after a subscriber action, such as downloading a whitepaper or attending a webinar.

An example of a nurture campaign would be a *follow-up series.* This may be triggered after a subscriber attends a webinar about a certain business product or service. A follow-up series of emails could highlight the features and benefits of that product or service and then offer a free trial or discount.

Marketers should also consider implementing nurture campaigns around areas of their buying cycles where subscribers tend to struggle or drop off. If marketers can provide informative content that helps recipients better understand their products or services, the better chance they have of getting potential buyers through those problem points and closer to purchase.

Content Stories for Automated Campaigns

When creating automated campaigns, marketers always struggle with content. How should it be prepared, and how should it progress from email to email?

To answer this, first start with your goal for that series of communications. Are you trying to educate only, encourage an action, sell, or up-sell to the contact? Whatever your goal, consider what steps the user has to take to reach that goal, what challenges they'll face along the way, and what incentives will work to help them get there. Then build a "content story" that will lead the recipient through that process.

Think of a content story like a TV show that plays out over a season (or several seasons). In each episode you'll learn more about each character, the story will progress and there will be milestones along the way. Treat your email the same way. Introduce content, evolve it, supplement it, and keep progressing toward a final conclusion.

Automated Campaign Frequency

When implementing automated campaigns, determining proper frequency is another big challenge and sits along with content development as being the biggest obstacle in creating a successful automated email campaign. Determining a proper frequency will take time, and it will vary from business to business. Your business type, how appropriate your content is, the content story you are telling, and other factors will all play into determining the right pacing for your messages.

However, there are some common traits among automated campaigns targeted at new leads.

Phase One: Build Value & Trust

In this phase you want to give as much as possible. Don't pitch or sell. Inform and educate. Let the recipient know you value the relationship and that you're THE expert in your industry.

- The email series should be between four and eight emails.
- Email every two to three days.
- Provide valuable content that educates and informs.
- Do not include sales pitches.

Phase Two: Engage

In this phase you want to deepen the relationship and encourage engagement. Have the user respond in some way to your messages.

- The email series should be three to six emails.
- Email less frequently, roughly once per week.
- Encourage engagement. Ask them to take a survey, share content on social channels, leave a comment or feedback, etc.
- It's okay to make a light offer at the end of the phase (just nothing too aggressive).

Phase Three: Establish the Relationship

The third phase is all about cementing the relationship. Those that are still expressing interest in your campaigns through opens, clicks, or other actions are valuable leads. At this point you want to deepen the relationship and encourage a committed response. A goal might be contacting a representative or asking for a proposal or quote.

- The email series should be three to five emails.
- Email once every five to ten days.
- Ask for a committed response at the end of the phase.

Marketing Automation Software

The use of marketing automation software has been growing significantly in recent years because marketers can increase

---

TAKEAWAY

Because the relationship is new, you want to reach out to them frequently, so you learn more about the subscriber. And as you are doing so, your content will introduce your brand, provide educational content, and ultimately cement that business relationship so that you're top of mind when they're ready to purchase.

operational efficiencies and increase revenue. Marketing automation software refers to a platform that is used to streamline, execute, and measure repetitive marketing tasks. Once something that only top brands could employ, it is now being executed by B2B marketers across all business types and skill levels.

> STAT
>
> **Email marketing is currently the top marketing automation feature.[74] 89% of marketers use email in their marketing automation platforms. Other top features include lead nurturing (84%), cross-channel campaign management (82%), and integrations such as CRM, mobile, social, etc. for accumulating customer intelligence (80%).**

Tasks to Automate

Along with automating various tasks, automation platforms also incorporate lots of other features including data management, CRM integration, resource management, campaign publishing, or delivery and analytics. Many marketing automation platforms provide a cross-channel feature set that integrates email marketing with other marketing channels including websites, social media, display advertising, mobile marketing, and more.

Many marketers are able to achieve success without marketing automation, but automation platform technology allows marketers to "think big" and exponentially increase the scale of their marketing efforts. Marketing automation processes enable and automate many modern marketing practices including:

- Lead generation
- Lead nurturing
- Segmentation
- Personalization
- Retention
- ROI measurement

Marketers who use automated messaging are able to program each element of the campaign including the following:

- The event (user action or specified time) that initiates the delivery of an email
- The periods of time for the scheduling and initiation of message deliveries
- The subject line, from name, from email, and content of the message

PART FOUR: Know Your Audience: Deliver Relevance

- The individual or group of contacts that should receive the automated message
- The cadence of messages in an automated campaign sequence, often called a "track"
- The number of messages in a track

Common types of automated email messages include:

- Welcome messages
- Confirmation or "thank you" emails
- Birthday or anniversary messages
- Upsell or cross-sell (suggested next purchase)
- New product or service announcements based on prior purchase or behavioral history
- Educational messaging
- Lead nurturing series
- Retention emails, such as renewal messages
- Alerts (products now in stock or available in your region)

Through the use of marketing automation software, marketers will find that they will be in better position to manage, nurture, and score leads effectively and eventually hand them off to sales. It also allows marketers to more easily determine which programs are working (or not working) and prove the effectiveness of those campaigns as they relate to generating leads or sales or through customer retention.

For email marketers, marketing automation tools implement many of the features of an email service provider and marry those with marketing capabilities in other channels. Email then becomes part of the bigger marketing picture, and more easily integrates with those other channels.

Automation Headaches

As much as automation tools can help the marketing process, they also come with their own set of headaches. Marketers need to realize that automation can play havoc with frequency. Marketers should be mindful of how many emails are sent, both from campaigns and automation, over a period of time. Many automation platforms will allow marketers to manage frequency and prioritize messaging. Marketers will need to pay special attention to this in order to avoid over-saturating their recipients' inboxes with too many marketing messages.

How do you know if you're ready to move beyond an email-centric platform and into a marketing automation platform? Consider the following:

1. Is your lead nurturing process complicated?
2. Do you require a lot of touch points to move a prospect through your sales cycle?
3. Does your marketing require significant amounts of personalization and segmentation?
4. Do you want to be able to filter leads based on activity and engagement?
5. Do you have more leads than your marketing and sales teams can manage effectively?
6. Do you need to quantify the value of your marketing programs to senior management?
7. Are you exhausting the capabilities of your email service provider?
8. Do data and analytics play a big role in your marketing efforts and decision-making process?

If you answered "yes" to most of these questions then you should explore a marketing automation platform. Automation platforms tend to cost more than an email-centric platform, but the additional functionality and the success you can realize from your marketing efforts will likely offset the platform investment.

Winner's Circle
- Automated email campaigns have many benefits including reduced manual processes, timely communications, streamlined lead-nurturing process, and ensured regular communication with contacts.
- Approach automated campaigns in phases. First build trust through information and education, then engage the recipient, and then ask for a committed response such as contacting a rep or requesting a quote.
- Consider moving from an email-centric platform to a marketing automation platform if your campaigns are complex with lots of touch points and if they include personalization, segmentation, and the need to filter based on activity and engagement.

PART FIVE:
Analysis:
Review, Revise, Results

How To Win At B2B Email Marketing

CHAPTER 19
Testing

Starting Line

In this chapter you will learn:
- Why testing is necessary to win at email marketing
- What campaign elements are the most popular to test
- How to test using A/B testing and multivariate testing
- What to test to increase revenue, click-throughs, or opens
- What to do after you test

You can't win at email marketing if you don't test. Testing is a step that all marketers should embrace.

Every campaign should be looked at from a testing methodology. Each campaign should be planned with a test in mind. At the most basic level, comparing one campaign to another campaign can highlight differences in performance. But smart marketers will test various components of their campaigns to determine what types of messaging or content resonates best with their audiences.

What Should You Test?

A typical email marketing goal is to increase conversions, but it may also be to improve brand perception or to educate recipients.

The most common email campaign elements that marketers test include:[75]

- Subject line (72%)
- Message (61%)
- Layout and images (50%)
- Call-to-action (50%)
- Days of the week sent (39%)
- Personalization (34%)
- Landing page (32%)
- Target audience (30%)
- From name (26%)

TAKEAWAY

Testing is your secret to success. Without conducting tests you can't improve or optimize your email marketing.

TIP

The goal of testing is to get the best performance possible out of your recipient database. You should always approach testing with a goal in mind.

PART FIVE: Analysis: Review, Revise, Results

It's not a coincidence that the easiest things to test are the most tested. Modifying the length or contents of your subject line is not difficult, and changing out message, layout, and call to action are relatively painless. Personalization and audience targeting are tested less, but testing those might result in a more dramatic change in campaign metrics.

When you approach testing, think about what you are trying to achieve. Try testing what you believe will have the most impact on your goals. If you are trying to increase sales, testing a price or special offer will likely have more impact than the color of your call-to-action button.

Types of Testing

A/B Testing

A/B Testing, sometimes referred to as split testing, is a methodology in which two variants (A and B, which represent the control and a variant) are tested to determine how they affect user behavior. The two versions need to be identical except for one variation. Version A is typically a standard email message that represents the control, while Version B is modified in some way.

Example: A B2B company with a customer list of 35,000 records creates an email campaign showcasing its newly upgraded software platform. The company traditionally uses a 15%-off discount on upgrade offers but wants to test if a different offer would resonate more with its audience. The company's marketing team members are curious whether a discounted price or free support makes a bigger impact on conversions.

- To 5,000 customers they send an email with an upgrade offer of 15% off.
- To another 5,000 customers they send an email with an upgrade offer that includes one year of free support.
- The rest of the email is identical in every way except for the offer.
- The company then monitors which offer drives more clicks to the website and which generates more sales. The one that generates more sales will then be sent to the remaining 25,000 contacts.

The purpose of the test was to determine which offer generated the most interest (clicks) and the most revenue (sales conversions).

It's possible that one offer may have generated more interest but less revenue. If so, the senders will learn which offer captured the attention of their audience and which offer drove recipients to purchase. And since they're only testing two variables, they must also consider that the winning version could still be the best of two underperforming options. Marketers should always run multiple A/B tests on a variety of variables to understand if those changes will improve their campaigns.

> STAT Only 30% of marketers conduct A/B testing and only 27% use multivariate testing.[76]

Multivariate Testing

Your email contact list probably includes a diverse audience, so creating campaigns that appeal to everyone is unrealistic. But identifying what elements and what combination of elements in your email work best is helpful as it will result in higher performing campaigns. That's where multivariate testing comes in.

While A/B testing allows marketers to test two variants, multivariate testing allows marketers to test multiple variations at the same time. There's no limit to how many variables can be tested, but marketers need to make sure they don't test so many that they can't achieve a statistically valid sample size for each variation. As a rule of thumb, you'll want at least 1,000 recipients testing each variation. If you have less than that you can still test, but unless you have more than a 20% variance between versions your results should not be considered conclusive.

Multivariate testing is typically employed to determine which combination of content and creative produces the best results. Multiple variables are tested at one time—copy, offer, design, time of delivery, etc.—and all the results of the various combinations are analyzed to determine which combination best achieves marketing goals.

By allowing for so many testing options, multivariate testing can accelerate your campaign optimization process. You can find the optimal setting more quickly, and the faster you determine this, the sooner you'll see improved results.

PART FIVE: Analysis: Review, Revise, Results

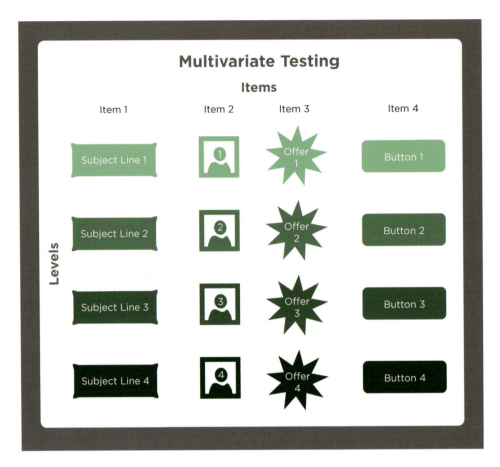

How to Conduct a Multivariate Test

Step 1: Determine what you want to test. Review your email campaigns to determine what elements you want to improve. Subject lines, images, call-to-action, layout, colors, etc., can all be variations in your multivariate test.

Step 2: Create the variations. Produce the various elements needed for the test. Write the copy changes and subject lines, or create the new images or buttons.

Step 3: Run the test. Use your email delivery platform to send the campaign. If your email marketing platform does not support multivariate testing, you can also create each variation yourself and send each to a portion of your list. This may not be possible if you have a lot of variations, but if you are only running eight to sixteen combinations, it may be within reason.

Step 4: Analyze the results. Monitor open rates, click rates, and conversions to determine which of the variations performed best.

CASE STUDY:

Act-On Software: **Responsive Design A/B Testing Leads to a 130% Increase in Clicks**

The rise in mobile email opens has led many brands to reconsider their email development strategies. Should you redesign and reprogram your emails to make them mobile friendly? Should you use responsive design? Does responsive design increase email engagement and, ultimately, sales ready leads (SRLs)?

Act-On Software hypothesized that responsive design would generate better results, but wanted to put it to a test. Act-On decided on an A/B test between its existing email layout, which was a straightforward non-mobile optimized HTML design, and a responsive email, which was optimized for mobile recipients.

THE CONTROL: Desktop View

PART FIVE: Analysis: Review, Revise, Results

The control included a bulletproof button for the call-to-action ("Download the Toolkit"). The image also linked to the landing page. The mobile version had display issues as the message extended beyond the viewable pane, the call-to-action was not visible above the fold, and the text was displayed in a small font.

THE TEST:
RESPONSIVE DESIGN

Both emails had similar content and the same subject line and from name; however, the responsive version is all text with a call-to-action. The large image has been removed and the email copy has been simplified.

THE CONTROL: Mobile View

THE TEST: Desktop View

168

How To Win At B2B Email Marketing

THE TEST: Mobile View

For the test, Act-On segmented 40,000 contacts from its "top of the funnel" list that had not participated in any marketing activities within the last 90 days. All contacts in the segment had marketing job titles. They were divided into two groups of 20,000 contacts each. One segment received Version A (control) and one segment received Version B (test). The emails were sent 15 minutes apart on a Wednesday morning.

When Act-On analyzed the results, there was a significant difference between the two versions. **The test version had a 130% increase in clicks and a 93.3% increase in SRLs.**

	Version A (Control)	Version B (Test)
Final Sent	19,462	19,211
Open Rate	5.1%	4.4%
Click Rate	5.0%	11.5%
SRLs	30	58

So why were the results so drastically different? Even with a lower open rate, the responsive design version was clearly the winner in click rate (by more than double) and SRLs (nearly double). The responsive email was simply easier to interact with on a mobile device, and that lead to recipients following through on the message.

As a result of the outcome of this test, Act-On has converted all its marketing emails to responsive.

This case study was originally prepared by Litmus. This version has been edited to include key points about the email testing procedure. View the entire case study at http://b2bemailmarketingbook.com/resources.

PART FIVE: Analysis: Review, Revise, Results

Things to Test

TIP

Increasing opens and clicks should be secondary to increasing conversions.

TIP

When it comes to the success of your campaigns, it's all about the offer.

Winning marketers test, test, and test some more. Because marketers can test so many variables, the best way to prioritize them is to start with the items that most impact your business. And that usually comes down to driving revenue.

An email with terrible copy and a horrid design will still generate lots of conversions if it includes an 80%-off offer. Likewise, a beautiful email with lots of great copy and a weak 5%-off offer will have a weak conversion rate.

When you plan your campaign, plan two or more distinct offer options and build your emails (and landing pages) around those offers. By testing in this manner you'll learn which kinds of offers drive the most conversions and gain insight on which offers capture the interest of your subscribers.

Once you've learned which offers generate the most revenue, then step back and try to increase click-throughs. The first place to start click-through testing is with the call-to-action. Test its copy, placement, and design.

After you have your offer and click-throughs optimized, then start testing items that drive increases in open rates. Open rates are determined by your subject line, from name, and preheader since that's what appears in the recipient's inbox.

You can test other things too, such as time and day of delivery, as that may impact all metrics (opens, clicks, and conversions).

Here's a full list of things to test.

To Increase Revenue

1. Offer copy and placement. Your offer is key to the success of your campaign. Test multiple offers and see what works best.

2. Landing page. A landing page can make or break an email campaign, so don't consider it secondary to your email message. The landing page should be a natural extension of the email itself and should provide an easy path to conversion.

3. List segmentation. Sending the right message to the right audience gets results. So break down your list by demographic, geographic, or other segments; create tests for each; and then determine what message works best for each segment. The more relevant you can make your message to the recipient, the more likely they'll generate a conversion.

4. Personalization. In order to produce a message that speaks to each recipient on an individual level, you'll need to personalize it with data from their records or content that speaks to their interests. Test using data-merge fields and targeted content to determine how much impact it has on engagement and conversions. This test can be done in both the subject line (to increase opens) and message body (to increase click-throughs).

To Increase Click-Throughs

1. Call-to-action copy, placement, and design. Your call-to-action (CTA) can have a profound effect on whether or not recipients click-through to your website or landing page. Test your call-to-action by creating CTA's that provide a benefit (continue learning), create urgency (sign up today only!), or provide a reward (free trial).

2. Creative. Don't just test minor creative elements; test entirely new creative concepts. Testing two or more email designs that include different headers, colors, fonts, and copy treatment will help you determine the creative the audiences like best. Remember that your creative tests should be in the same layout if you want to focus on only testing creative impact.

3. Layout. With the wide range of devices being used to access email, it's important that you test your layout to determine what works best for your audience. Try different layouts with your content, different placements for your call to action, and other changes to the placement of items in your messages.

4. Preview pane view. Even with a growing mobile audience, the preview pane is still an important item to test. Desktop users, which still represent a significant portion of your recipients, will see the top or upper left portion of your email while they are going through their inbox. If you optimize your message and offer so that it appears in that preview page space, you'll generate more interest from your recipients.

5. Message copy. Message copy can be an easily overlooked part of your testing process. But test your greeting, body, and closing along with length of copy to see what works best. Sometimes longer copy creates more impact, but if it doesn't, keep your messages short and sweet (especially if you have a large mobile-recipient base).

6. Design elements. You can test the impact of visual items within your message such as buttons, images/photos, fonts, color schemes, etc. Running a multivariate test with different variations of design elements can quickly help you learn which ones (if any) create any significant impact.

7. Animated GIFs. Try adding animation to your email and test it compared to emails without animation. Sometimes a little movement can increase interest and result in additional click-throughs.

To Increase Opens

1. Subject line. Subject lines can determine whether your message is opened or deleted. Test both the phrasing and language of your subject line, and test what length works best. You may also want to test using character symbols to see if they impact open rates.

And as a word of caution: if you test subject lines with different offers, realize that the offer will impact opens as much as a change in the subject line language or length. If you are testing subject lines only, use the same offer.

2. From name. Test whether a company name (ACME Products), a personal name (John Sample), or a combination of the two (John Sample of ACME Products) generates opens. Others have also tested using an email address as a from name and adding a phone number to the from name field. Adding a phone number should only be used in the from name if your goal is generating a phone conversation.

To Increase Revenue, Click-Throughs, or Opens

1. Time of send. Stagger your email campaigns, so they are sent at various timeframes throughout the day (or possibly only during business hours). You'll want to keep the timeframes to hourly or some other small segment. Then break down the opens, clicks, and conversions within each hour to determine when your audience is most responsive.

2. Day of send. Break down your list into five or seven segments, and send to one segment each weekday or day of the week. Review what days generate the most activity. Don't be afraid to test sending business emails before or after work hours and even on weekends. Some businesses have found that abnormal send times help them stand out from the competition.

3. Delivery by time zone. If you have the ability to send as a batch versus sending at times based on time zone, test the two and see if delivering at consistent times across time zones improves any measurable metrics.

Running a test once is not enough to make an important decision. Run tests multiple times to ensure the accuracy of your results.

After the Test

Once you've run A/B or multivariate testing, make sure you have a plan to implement what you've learned from your testing by modifying your campaigns. Work with your marketing and sales teams to help them understand results, and then prepare campaigns that demonstrate those lessons by putting the results into action.

Have some fun with your testing too. Before the campaign goes out try to predict the results you'll achieve. You'll likely be surprised by some of the results you encounter. Testing almost always reveals a few secrets and creates many surprises. Sometimes big changes that you think will generate a large impact will barely move the needle, while small changes may generate big results.

Testing is widely considered the most important tactic to use to improve your email marketing, so always test and re-test, and never settle by thinking you've achieved the maximum results. Constant improvement should be your goal, and testing is the best way to identify areas for improvement.

Testing is all about learning. Learning what works and what doesn't work. Test anything that you think will effect change, and learn how your audience reacts. Then continue to carry on with what you've learned while testing additional elements. Before you know it you'll have lots of data to help you optimize your future campaigns.

Winner's Circle
- Testing is your secret to success. Without conducting tests you can't improve or optimize your email marketing.
- The goal of testing is to get the best performance possible out of your recipient database. You should always approach testing with a goal in mind.
- Use A/B testing to test one element in your campaign, or use multivariate testing to test multiple elements.
- Try testing different elements to increase revenue, click-throughs, or opens.
- After the test, analyze your results and have a plan to implement what you've learned.

PART FIVE: Analysis: Review, Revise, Results

CHAPTER 20
Metrics: Analyze and Win

Starting Line

In this chapter you will learn:
- Why winning marketers always review campaign metrics
- Which metrics drive success and which ones are indicators of potential success
- What the definitions and metrics calculations are for delivery, open, click, evaluation, and website effectiveness
- How to determine financial metrics to understand how much revenue is generated from your email marketing efforts

TAKEAWAY

Winning marketers evaluate campaign performance, understand how it performed against business goals, and use the lessons from campaign reports to improve their future marketing efforts.

Your email campaign doesn't end when you hit the send button. Reviewing campaign performance is a must for any serious marketer. If you don't understand how well your campaign performed and if you don't learn from your campaign's weaknesses, then you will not be able to make changes and improve your future marketing efforts.

Your entire campaign should be built toward achieving a business goal. In the end, nothing else matters unless you are meeting those business objectives.

Indicators and Results Drivers

If you review your email marketing reports, it's very likely that you are tracking metrics that don't matter. Which metrics are meaningless? Any metric that provides no data on business success.

When you start digging into your campaign reports you'll begin to understand which metrics drive success and which ones are *indicators of potential success.* You should pay attention to indicators as improving them will likely lead to better results.

TAKEAWAY

In the end, the only metrics that matter are the ones that positively impact your business.

PART FIVE: Analysis: Review, Revise, Results

Email open rates are a good example of an indicator. You obviously want recipients to open your emails, and it's necessary for a recipient to open an email for them to take action on your message.

TAKEAWAY

Standard metrics like opens and clicks are useful indicators, but make sure you focus your attention on analytics that lead to fulfilling your business objectives.

But does a higher open rate always result in more conversions? What if your email has a great subject line but has poorly written copy and a bad layout or lacks a call to action? That will likely result in a lot of opens but limited conversions.

If you have a campaign with limited opens but a great offer and lots of action toward conversions, you have a campaign with great business value. And if you could achieve even more opens and therefore more conversions, then you have a goal for your next campaign.

Analytics Data Sources

Campaign analysis is not just limited to the email. To get a true picture of the extent of your campaign success, you'll need to gather data from at least these sources:

1. Email campaign data. This will include delivery statistics, opens, clicks, forwards, unsubscribes, etc.

2. Website analytics. This will show you how many people visited your website and landing pages, and what actions and paths they took once they were there.

3. Business metrics. In order to truly understand campaign success, you may need to know other metrics including customer lifetime value, average purchase price, average lead conversion percentage, etc.

You'll need to make plans prior to the start of your campaign so that you can set up tracking or gather data on any metrics that matter. You must add the unique URLs, tracking pixels, or any other tracking mechanisms to your website, and gather your business metrics data prior to campaign delivery to get the full picture of your campaign value.

Evolve Beyond the Open: Metrics You Need To Know

While opens and clicks are metrics you should track, they are not the only metrics you want to track. Day and time of delivery, clicked links, the path email click-through visitors took on your website, and other more-advanced data will provide the insight you need to truly gauge the effectiveness of your campaigns.

Which metrics are worth your time? That'll depend on your business. But here's a review of the metrics you should consider when analyzing your email campaign.

Note: the majority of these metrics are defined by the Digital Marketing Association's (DMA) Email Experience Council in the Support the Adoption of Metrics for Email (The S.A.M.E.) Project, which outlined these measurement standards in June 2010.[77]

Delivery Metrics

Accepted: any email that is not rejected by a server, including emails delivered to the inbox, spam, or junk folders; *accepted = sent – bounced.*

Accepted rate: the total amount successfully delivered to the server divided by the total email deployed (unique records); *accepted emails / sent emails = accepted rate.*

Bounce: a message rejected by the receiving server. Typically bounces are referred to as either a hard bounce (a delivery failure for permanent reason, e.g., a misspelled email address), or a soft bounce (a delivery failure due to a temporary condition, e.g., mailbox is currently full).

Inbox placement rate: the ratio of emails that are delivered specifically to the recipient's inbox divided by the total emails sent; *inbox placement rate = emails sent that reached inbox / number of emails sent.*

Open Metrics

Confirmed open rate: the percentage of unique confirmed opens divided by the total number of accepted emails; *confirmed opens / accepted = confirmed open rate.*

Unique confirmed opens: the unique number of users to whom an email is displayed (whether fully opened or within the preview pane) and recorded; includes both HTML and plain text email; *unique confirmed opens / accepted = unique confirmed open rate.* The unique confirmed open rate will provide insight on the interest level of your recipients. From name recognition, subject line, and preheader quality (or lack thereof) will directly affect the unique confirmed open rate.

Total confirmed opens: the total number of times an email is displayed (whether displayed in the preview pane or fully opened) and recorded using a tracking image OR if the user clicks any link including the unsubscribe link; *total confirmed opens / accepted = total confirmed open rate.*

Email render rate: a percentage expressing the number of times an email is displayed (whether displayed in the preview pane or fully opened), which is recorded using a tracking image within an HTML formatted message; the total renders divided by the total and expressed as a percentage; *email renders / accepted emails = render rate.*

Unique email render: the unique number of users to whom an email is displayed (whether displayed in the preview pane or fully opened), which is recorded using tracking image; *unique email renders / accepted emails = unique render rate.* If a user opens the email multiple times or if multiple tracking pixels requests are recorded due to forwarding, only one is counted per unique email address. This metric applies to HTML formatted emails only.

Total emails rendered: the total number of times an email is displayed (whether displayed in the preview pane or fully opened), which is recorded using only a tracking pixel for a unique subscriber address; *total email renders / accepted emails = total render rate.* If the user opens the email multiple times, one email render is counted for each occurrence. This metric is based off of HTML formatted emails only.

Average recipient render rate: the total number of times an email is rendered (whether displayed in the preview pane or fully opened), which is captured using a tracking image within an HTML format message divided by the unique number of emails rendered, expressed as a percentage; *total renders / unique renders = average recipient render rate.*

Average recipient render rate provides insight into the average number of times each recipient views an individual message. This may be of value to marketers with longer-format content or content that has a long shelf life (e.g. newsletters). A higher rate may indicate that recipients found the content useful and revisited it multiple times.

Click Metrics

Click-through rate (CTR): the number of times a link is clicked from a message divided by the number of accepted messages; *clicks / accepted emails = click-through rate.* For example, consider an email sent to four people where two of the recipients opened the message and one of the recipients clicks on a link. The resulting CTR for that link is 25% (1 unique clicker / 4 accepted emails = 25%). This metric may be calculated as **unique CTR**, which refers to the number of people that clicked. It can also be calculated as **total CTR**, which refers to number of clicks for a specific link.

Email marketers also often calculate CTR for the entire email to compare several emails within a campaign or across campaigns.

Click-to-open (CTO) rate: the unique number of times a link is clicked from a message divided by the unique number of confirmed opens for that message; *clicks / email renders = click-to-open rate*. If a message is sent to four people, two people render the email, and one of those people clicks on a link one or more times, the resulting CTO is 50% (1 click / 2 confirmed opens = 50%). Again, this metric may be calculated as **unique CTO referring** to the number of people that clicked or **total CTO** referring to number of clicks for a specific link. The click-to-open rate may also be calculated for the entire email rather than an individual link.

Evaluation Metrics

Once you've learned and used the standard email marketing metrics, you may want to add some additional formulas to your analytics review process. These additional formulas may assist with campaign performance evaluation and help determine business value from your marketing campaign.

Click-to-accepted rate (CTAR): the number of clicks from your email campaign divided by the number of emails accepted (not sent); *number of clicks / number of emails accepted = click-to-accepted rate*. This metric can help you measure the quality of your email list and how well your message is received by your recipients. More recipients clicking from your email to follow through on your offer shows how well your marketing message resonates and how receptive your audience is to receiving AND ACTING on your message.

You can also use CTAR to help identify quality segments within your list. Break your list apart by any demographic and determine the CTAR rate, and then see which audience segments respond best to your messaging.

Click reach: the number of unique first-time clicks from your email campaigns over a period of time. To figure out click reach, take the total clicks over a series of campaigns, and remove any clicks by users that clicked two or more times. Take the total number of unique first-time clicks and divide it by the average send quantity (the total send quantity of all your campaigns divided by the number of campaigns) of the same series of campaigns to determine the click-reach percentage.

The click reach will help you understand what your total reach is over time, and whether or not the same recipients always click or if you have a broad range of recipients that click-through on your marketing messages.

Recipient retention rate (RRR): the rate at which recipients are kept from one campaign to the next; *number of subscribers - bounce backs - unsubscribes / number of subscribers = recipient retention rate*. Recipients may be removed due to bounce backs or unsubscribes.

Your recipient retention rate is a combination of list quality and marketing effectiveness. If your list does not produce many bounce backs (high accepted rate) and does not produce many unsubscribes (a measure that people like your marketing content) then your recipient retention rate should be closer to 100%.

Many email records will simply become invalid over time, so expect that certain things outside of your control will contribute to this metric. But watching this metric for anomalies or fluctuations can help you determine when there's reason for concern.

Website Effectiveness Metrics

Many email marketers only look at the success of their email program, but if you are getting clicks to your website and not getting conversions, then you are devaluing the strength of your email campaigns. The website has to cash the checks that your email delivers.

Evaluating website analytics along with your email campaigns will provide a deep dive into the overall effectiveness of your campaigns and potentially show areas where drop-off occurs. Learning about these weak links can help you identify your biggest obstacles, and fixing those can lead to greatly improved results.

Open-to-conversion rate (OTCR): *number of opens / number of conversions = open-to-conversion rate.*

Click-to-conversion rate (CTCR): *number of clicks / number of conversions = click-to-conversion rate.*

A conversion is the desired outcome from your email campaign. It could be an e-commerce purchase, a white paper download, a webinar registration, completing a web form, or many other things. In order to track these conversion rates, you must be able to track conversions on your website. Step one is to make sure you have that in place or that you can access that data via your IT or web team.

The open-to-conversion rate (OTCR) typically shows the effectiveness and value of your offer. If subscribers opened the email, clicked through, and converted, then the recipient found enough value in your marketing message to follow through to conversion.

Because the subscriber has to take two or more actions from the open to the conversion (open email, click through to website, convert on website), this metric is more of an overview of the entire process of everyone that originally expressed interest in your message (by opening it). Treat it as such.

The click-to-conversion rate (CTCR) shows how effective your website is at allowing visitors from email campaigns to complete a conversion. Because this metric is determined after a recipient leaves the email, it can highlight whether or not your website is helping or hurting your conversion process.

The CTCR may be best determined by analyzing clicks from particular links in your campaign (the CTA) and not from ALL clicks as that will better show the outcome rate of those that took action on your intended offer (and eliminate non-marketing focused clicks such as view online, edit profile, etc.)

Micro-Conversions

You may also want to track micro-conversions as they will also show additional value from your email marketing efforts. Micro-conversions can be added value conversions such as newsletter opt-ins, new social media connections, form completions, etc.

Open-to-micro-conversion rate (OTMCR): *number of opens / number of micro-conversions = open-to-micro-conversion rate.*

PART FIVE: Analysis: Review, Revise, Results

Click-to-micro-conversion rate (CTMCR): *number of clicks / number of micro-conversions = click to micro-conversion rate.*

Click-to-page-view rate: tracking page views on your website can help you identify the weakest points in the path to conversion; *number of clicks / number of page views = click-to-page-view rate.*

A typical email conversion process is when the recipient goes from email to landing page to product/service page to conversion page (form, checkout, etc.). Additional page views may happen in between, or it is possible a conversion can happen right from the landing page. But whatever the situation, set yourself up so that you can track page views of each web page that originated from the email.

Once you have your tracking in place, you can look at each step of the process and see where drop-off occurred. Did 75% of your click-throughs not make it past the landing page? Maybe your landing page needs some work. Did 95% of landing page visitors go to the download form but only 20% fill it out? Maybe your download form is too long or the offer is not compelling. This is the kind of valuable insight your page-views metrics can help you identify.

Financial Metrics

While opens, clicks, and conversions are all important, the most important metric is understanding how much revenue is generated as a direct result of your email marketing efforts.

To determine revenue metrics you'll first need to know your overall revenue and your campaign costs.

Total campaign revenue: the total campaign revenue is the monetary value of all conversions AND micro-conversions.

Conversions are likely easy to determine as purchases, leads, or other business goals may already be tracked by your organization.

However, don't forget that some micro-conversions can be expressed as monetary value too. If your business has determined that one out of every 50 new opt-ins eventually becomes a customer, then you can take the average lifetime value of a customer and divide it by 50 to show the average value of a new opt-in contact.

Also consider that your campaign revenue may be determined by short-term and long-term value. A new customer may purchase X as a direct result of your campaign, but may have a lifetime value worth

10 times the original purchase. So consider how your business should factor in lifetime value when determining campaign revenue metrics.

Total campaign cost: the total campaign cost is the cost of ALL expenses for the campaign including resources, overhead, production costs, assets, platform fees, bandwidth and server costs, etc.

Once you understand total campaign revenue and cost, you can apply that to your campaign metrics.

Average revenue per email sent: the total revenue generated as a direct result of your email campaigns divided by the number of emails sent; *total campaign revenue / number of emails sent = average revenue per email sent.*

This metric will be a solid indicator of the overall productivity of your email campaign. In order to have quality average revenue per email sent numbers, you'll need to have quality deliverability, open rates, click rates, and conversion rates. Improvements in this metric tend to be an indicator of improvements in the campaign as a whole.

Marketers can change this metric to eliminate weak areas of their campaigns by determining average revenue per email delivered or average revenue per email opened. However, by doing so they're not getting a true representation of the effectiveness of the entire campaign.

Achieving high average revenue per email sent numbers will require a clean list, good deliverability, effective targeting, an actionable offer, high engagement and response rates, etc.

Campaign profitability: subtract the costs of the goods sold and the total campaign cost from the total campaign revenue to determine campaign profitability; *total campaign revenue - total campaign cost - cost of goods sold = campaign profitability.*

Many marketers will measure total campaign revenue but never consider the costs associated with the campaign creation, execution, and fulfillment. In many cases, this is due to the difficulty in determining the campaign costs and cost of goods sold.

Marketers may need to work with their finance or sales groups to learn this information, but it is necessary if businesses truly want to see how their marketing impacts the bottom line. An email campaign with high conversion numbers can be an unsuccessful business effort if the campaign costs and costs of goods sold exceed the campaign

PART FIVE: Analysis: Review, Revise, Results

revenue. That can work in the other direction too—a campaign with low conversion rates can still be considered a business success if the campaign costs and costs of goods sold is lower than the campaign revenue.

Average annual value of an email address: divide your annual revenue from email by your average list size to determine your average annual value of an email address; *annual revenue from email / average list size = average annual value of an email address.*

This metric is fairly easy to determine, and it's a great metric to use to determine the maximum amount you should spend to acquire a new subscriber.

For example, if you earned $5 million in revenue from your email campaigns in the past year, and you have an average list size of 860,000 records, then your average annual value of an email address is $5.81. Therefore, you can safely spend up to $5.81 to acquire a new email address knowing that it will be profitable within one year's time.

This value is helpful for your marketing team who may be purchasing online ads and pay-per-click search or using inbound marketing as it will provide a financial ceiling to reference as they research media options.

Return on investment (ROI): Because this is the "golden metric" used by so many marketers, we'll explore this one in depth in the next chapter.

Winner's Circle
- Winning marketers evaluate campaign performance, understand how it performed against business goals, and use the lessons from campaign reports to improve their future marketing efforts.
- The only metrics that matter are the ones that positively impact your business.
- You will need more than email tracking data to fully analyze campaign results. Data from your website and other business metrics may be necessary to fully understand the value of the campaign.
- Review which metrics are important to your business, and track those from campaign to campaign. Always try to improve on those metrics.

How To Win At B2B Email Marketing

CHAPTER 21
Determining ROI

Starting Line

In this chapter you will learn:
- What ROI is and how it is calculated
- What the rules are for ROI
- How to generate better ROI
- What some common ROI challenges are and how to solve them

ROI = Return on Investment

Return on investment, often shortened to "ROI," is the value of what your business gets back from your marketing efforts. It determines how well your marketing is working. A positive ROI means you're getting results from your campaigns. Negative ROI means you're losing money, and your marketing efforts should be improved immediately.

Use the standard ROI calculation: (gain from investment - cost of investment) / cost of investment.

$$ROI = \frac{(\text{Gain from Investment} - \text{Cost of Investment})}{\text{Cost of Investment}}$$

For example, if you generate $3,500 from your campaign but spent $1,000 creating it, then you would your determine your ROI first by subtracting the cost of investment from your investment gain.

$3,500 - $1,000 = $2,500

Then take the $2,500 net gain and divide it by the cost of investment.

$2,500/$1,000 = 2.5

Your ROI is 2.5 times the cost of investment, or expressed as a percentage, is 250%.

PART FIVE: Analysis: Review, Revise, Results

ROI Rules

In order to determine true ROI, you must follow several rules. Taking shortcuts and not factoring in necessary costs can lead to incorrect calculations, and doing so will produce inaccurate results.

1. ROI is media-agnostic. If you produce content that is used only in your email newsletter, then the cost of generating that content must be factored into the email ROI calculation. Any costs associated with copywriting, graphic design, stock photography, research, testing, etc., must all be considered when calculating ROI.

2. Every resource has a value. The time spent by you or your staff creating the email content, developing the email campaign, managing recipient data, sending the campaign, etc., must all be considered in the email ROI calculation. You should know the hourly or daily costs of each person on your team, their overhead, the costs of your email service provider, etc., and factor all that into your ROI cost of investment.

TAKEAWAY

ROI cannot be expressed in numbers of new followers, likes, or page views.

3. ROI can only be calculated after the investment has yielded a return. You have to be able to show a positive return from your campaign before being able to calculate the campaign ROI. A campaign with zero return (or worse yet, a negative return) will obviously not yield a positive ROI.

4. ROI must be calculated in dollars. Return on investment is a monetary calculation.

ROI's Role in B2B Marketing

The good news is that many organizations perceive email marketing as a strong producer of ROI. The bad news is that many businesses don't know what value email is really providing their organizations. In the 2013 Email Marketing Benchmark Report, B2B marketers estimated that email marketing delivered a 127% ROI for their organizations.

That was higher than reported by B2C organization (114%) and those that do both B2B and B2C (108%).[78]

Marketers have also realized that email marketing can offer the highest ROI of any marketing channel. In 2012, email delivered an ROI of $39.40, easily beating search marketing ($22.24), display advertising ($19.72), social ($12.71) and mobile ($10.51). By 2016, the DMA estimates that email marketing will have a return on investment of $35.02.[79]

With this kind of ROI, email is far and away the best channel for marketers to use if they're interested in driving value to their businesses.

How to Generate Better ROI

1. All goals have value. Before you can generate a return on investment, you have to know what will lead to a positive return. For many companies that will be a sale. But other goals have value as well. If you know the value of an opt-in, a lead, or a retained client or customer, you can use those to calculate ROI too.

For example: if your business knows that on average one out of every 25 leads becomes a customer and that the lifetime value of the customer is $4,000, then you can value a new lead at $160. So if your $4,000 campaign results in 100 new leads, then you can calculate your campaign ROI: 100 new leads means four new customers. Four new customers are worth $16,000.

$16,000 - $4,000 = $12,000

$12,000 / $4,000 = 3

So your campaign's ROI was three times the cost of investment or 300%.

2. Design campaigns to be measurable. You can't calculate ROI if you can't measure results. You have to know how many goals were achieved as a result of your campaign.

Make sure you have tracking methods in place that can prove that a contact originated from your campaign. This may mean setting up click tracking, website tracking pixels, custom landing pages, referral codes, or identifying the source of the contact in your database or CRM platform.

3. Always test and analyze results. If the opportunity and timing exists, it's always advised to run a small test before launching the larger campaign. Open up the campaign to a limited audience, and then watch and analyze incoming metrics. Review your test campaign, make changes to improve results, and either test to a small audience again or launch the full campaign.

4. Focus on decisions that improve ROI. When reviewing and analyzing your campaign, always make changes that focus on improving the campaign's ROI. Keep in mind that this can be done by reducing costs as well as improving results.

ROI Challenges and Solutions

The biggest challenges of why businesses don't measure email ROI usually falls into one or more of several excuses. Let's call these excuses "challenges."

Challenge one: lack of knowledge on how to set up conversion tracking. Solution: work with your IT or web development team to set up conversion tracking from your email platform or track conversions using website analytics software.

Challenge two: lack of tracking ability from your email platform. Solution: upgrade your platform to one that provides conversion tracking capabilities.

Challenge three: your business doesn't know customer costs or order value. Solution: your sales team should already have this data. If not, ask your sales team to determine these numbers.

Challenge four: lack of agreement on marketing goals. Solution: confusion often occurs because there are multiple goals for most marketing campaigns. Retention, up-sell, engagement, increasing brand awareness, etc., might all be "goals" of one marketing effort. During the planning phase, work with your marketing team to determine what goal or goals are most important, and focus your effort on goals that deliver the most business value.

Reporting to Senior Management

If you're going to connect with your C-suite, you'll need to put your results in a language they understand and manage a dialogue on their terms. And make sure you understand what they're looking for. The senior-level executives in your company are going to be much more impressed with figures that include dollar signs and even more impressed with figures that show positive value to the company. After all, linking marketing effectiveness to a positive financial performance is the ultimate goal for most marketers.

Winning Tactic #1: Understand leadership goals.

Know what your C-Suite is trying to achieve from a business perspective, and make sure your email marketing efforts are in sync with those objectives.

Winning Tactic #2: Identify how email marketing ROI achieves goals.

Use ROI metrics to show how marketing investments are working toward achieving the big-picture corporate goals. Make the C-Suite understand that your program is a valuable investment in realizing the corporate vision.

Winning Tactic #3: Outline how you can continue to improve results.

Show not only your successes but also how you plan to improve what you've already done. Make the C-Suite understand that email marketing expenses are already successful and that you have plenty of opportunity to increase ROI with their continued investment.

Winning Tactic #4: Show that your expenses lead to profit.

Senior management will frequently question business expenses and sometimes will do so without looking at the revenue it produces. In order to defend your expenses, make sure you highlight the revenue that is produced from those expenses, so management realizes that its investment in email is generating a positive business outcome.

The Problems with ROI

Even though ROI is considered one of the most important marketing metrics, there are several reasons why it may be wrong for measuring marketing impact. ROI is never considered a bad calculation, but many times it is relied upon to express marketing value when that's not how marketers are determining it.

Marketing Value Versus ROI

Marketing value is achieved through financial performance measures such as net profit. Net profit is realized by subtracting your marketing costs from the revenue. But ROI is expressed as a percentage that is derived by dividing your profit by your marketing expense. That difference of subtraction versus division is where some challenge the ROI equation and whether or not it is the best calculation to determine marketing value.

ROI Does Not Equal Profit

Return on investment and net profit are two different things. ROI deals with the financial commitment invested toward a business objective and the return you realized in revenue based on the net profit from that business. Profit, on the other hand, measures the financial performance of the business. So marketers shouldn't confuse ROI with profit. And, although uncommon, it is possible for efforts that achieve positive ROI to be unprofitable for a business.

ROI Doesn't Calculate Soft Benefits

ROI models don't have the ability to calculate soft benefits into the equation. Customer satisfaction, resource effectiveness, employee productivity, quality of technology, and other intangible items affect the potential for net profit but don't have a place in the ROI calculation.

If your campaign produced great ROI but did so at the expense of customer satisfaction or at the expense of achieving future profits, does that really result in an improvement for your business?

ROI Requires All Costs to Be Calculated

When determining the "cost of investment" part of the ROI calculation, many marketers are not able to truly identify all costs involved. Many marketers will guesstimate certain expenses, or will leave them out all together if it will benefit the end result. And because many of these expenses aren't really trackable by those who ultimately review the calculations, it's easy for marketers to swing ROI calculations in their favor.

ROI Misses the Big Picture

Positive ROI around a specific campaign or even a group of campaigns is worthless if the broader corporate marketing goals are not met.

Many marketers look at the ROI of a campaign or a smaller marketing initiative. And it's great to understand the value of that marketing effort, but if ROI is limited to these smaller segments, then it's only delivering an analysis of a small portion of your business.

Winner's Circle

- The ROI calculation is the gain from investment minus the cost of investment divided by the cost of investment.
- In order to determine ROI, you have to know the value of all goals that you achieve.
- Create campaigns that are measurable.
- When reviewing and analyzing a campaign, always make changes that focus on improving the campaign's ROI.
- If you are not measuring ROI, understand what challenges are creating issues and work to solve them.
- When reporting ROI to senior management, understand their goals and show how email marketing helps achieve them. Show that your expenses lead to a profit.

PART SIX:
The Future of B2B Email Marketing

Emerging Concepts in B2B Email Marketing
CHAPTER 22

Starting Line

In this chapter you will learn:
- How relevant B2B email marketing will be in five years
- What lies ahead in B2B email marketing technology, platforms, data, content, and design

Email marketing has come a long way since its inception in 1971. As a business tool, it's been an invaluable communication platform for businesses for over 20 years. So where will email go next? Is email heading downhill, or is there still room for growth?

In a B2B email marketing poll, respondents were asked how relevant email will be in five years. The results:[80]

- Still relevant: 47%
- Less relevant: 50%
- Not relevant: 3%

Even those who thought it would be "less relevant" didn't think it would be "not relevant." So 97% of marketers think that email marketing will have some relevance in five years. Maybe that's why businesses are increasing their investments in email.

Email leads all marketing channels in marketing budget growth. Some 61% of brands will increase email spending in 2015. That comes in ahead of social media (49%) and mobile marketing (40%).[81]

So what lies ahead for email? Will there be significant changes in the channel? What new features, technologies, or trends will emerge? Here are a few newer ideas that are already starting to make their way into email campaigns and may become the next new "big thing."

Dynamic/Agile/Real-Time Emails

We've been trained to think that an outgoing email message can't change once it's sent. But what if a message could change based on

PART SIX: The Future Of B2B Email Marketing

when or where the email is opened, or based on how the recipient interacts with the message?

This new concept of delivering agile, real-time content has the potential to change the way marketers and recipients think about email content. These new platforms allow marketers to change messages on the fly. By doing so, emails can be more agile, which can increase recipient interest and engagement.

When executed successfully, these messages take the concept of personalization to an entirely new level. Emails become more relevant and deliver better value to the recipient, which should delivery better ROI to the marketer.

One company providing this service now is Movable Ink. Its emails include real-time data (prices, stock quotes, weather, special offers, etc.), countdown timers, local maps, live Twitter feeds, device-specific actions, and more.

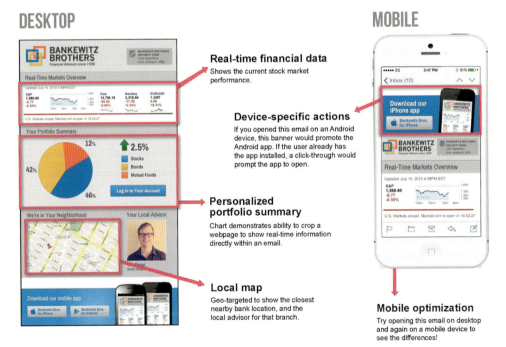

Fully Personalized Emails

Marketers have been moving away from batch-and-blast emails to more personalized emails for several years now. In the future, improvements in technology, data management, and automation will likely allow for many marketers to realize fully personalized emails. No email would be the same—each one would include content and offers fully customized for each recipient.

In fact, 78% of marketers believe that in the next five years, all email communication will be completely personalized.[82]

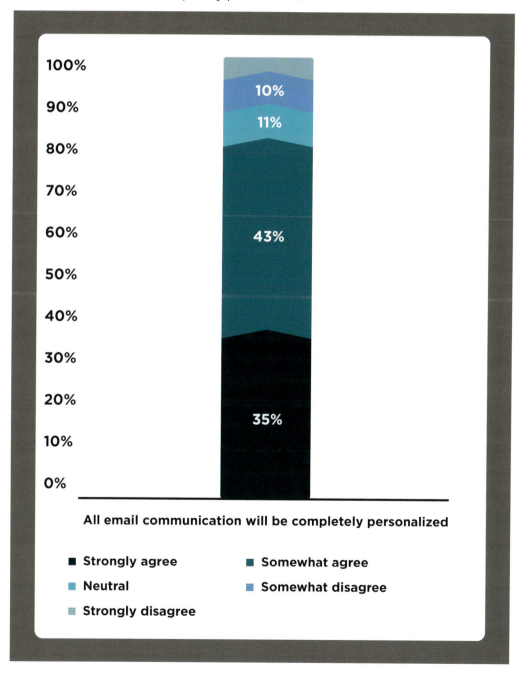

PART SIX: The Future Of B2B Email Marketing

In-Email Transactions

Since inception, in order to complete a transaction started by an email, a recipient would need to go to a website or take an appropriate offline action (store visit, phone call, etc.). However, it's now possible to complete a transaction without leaving your inbox. Companies like Striata (http://striata.com) allow for e-statements to be sent to the inbox and paid through a secure PDF attachment. And Rebelmail (http://rebelmail.com) provides a way for recipients to purchase items and make payments without leaving their mailboxes.

As email software gets better and more secure, it won't be long before more businesses take advantage of inbox transaction technology.

Cross-Channel Integration

Business professionals seek information across many marketing channels. And the growth of these additional channels means that email cannot stand alone. Effective email marketing should be integrated with an overall marketing approach.

Email needs to integrate with mobile, search, social, display, direct mail, and potentially several other marketing channels. Multi-channel marketing is no longer a novel idea— it is how businesses must operate if they want to remain competitive.

Companies that want to grow relationships with their contacts have to engage them cross-channel. Using tools that allow email to synchronize with campaigns in other platforms and track the results will become more important as marketers become more sophisticated. Marketers will realize that in order to stand out from the competition, they'll need to engage everywhere their prospect goes, and in many cases know that before the prospect gets there.

Will there be one platform that can integrate all marketing channels? In one study, 85% of respondents agreed there will be within the next five years.[83]

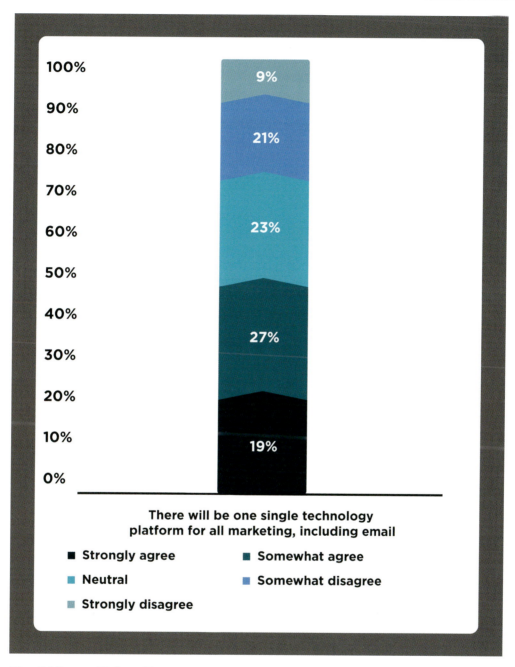

Putting Big Data to Use

The majority of B2B marketers give themselves low marks for their use of analytics data. Very few are putting their data to work. B2B email marketers should be using their email analytics, website analytics, and CRM data to help improve their marketing efforts.

For many, the challenge isn't gathering or accessing the data; it's digging into the data to understand what the data represents. CRM data can help marketers segment audiences. Email analytics data can help marketers determine which content recipients find most engaging. And website analytics data can show you what email recipients do after a click-through.

In the near future it's likely more marketers will become proficient at analyzing data, understanding it, and putting it to use for their business. If you haven't already, dive into your data to see what you find. You'll likely uncover key information or reveal secrets that have been hidden in your data files the entire time.

Micro-Segmentation

Segmentation is a popular email strategy, but many marketers want to take it a step further by creating very refined segments, usually based on several segmentation criteria. This micro-segmentation strategy will allow for marketers to target very focused audiences with very specific messages.

Because marketers are gaining access to more and more data, micro-segmentation may already be a tactic employed by savvy marketers and one that will eventually become standard practice as added data and better technology become commonplace.

HTML5

Many websites are now using HTML5 as it offers significant improvements over HTML4. HTML5 offers a more interactive and richer experience both from a design and programmatic standpoint.
Email marketers can find value in using HTML5 as well. While it's not standard practice yet, marketers are exploring how it can be used to deliver improvements to their campaigns.

Some of the benefits of HTML5 include:
1. Using layers of content and allowing individual layers to move or animate.
2. Better handling of audio and video, including video effects and streaming directly into an opened email
3. Animation capabilities.
4. The ability to hide and access content.

Many of the benefits of HTML5 are exactly what marketers want to use in their emails to create a more immersive and interactive experience. So why aren't more marketers using HTML5 in their email campaigns? Mostly because not all email clients support it. While most web browsers are now HTML5 compliant, some email platforms are not. Microsoft Outlook and Gmail are the biggest clients that don't offer HTML5 support, and until they do many marketers don't feel HTML5 is a viable option. Those audiences are just too large to take a gamble using a language that won't work properly for a large segment of the receiving audience.

So does HTML5 in email have a future? Probably, but only if email clients like Outlook and Gmail eventually support it and if all ISPs allow it to be used without altering or stripping elements of the code before it reaches the inbox.

So can you experiment with HTML5 now in your email campaigns? Sure. If you know that a recipient uses a certain email client that is HTML5 compatible, like Apple Mail, Outlook.com or an iOS device, you can prepare campaigns for that segment of your audience.

Audio and Video in Email

Does the idea of playing music or videos directly in an email sound too good to be true? Most marketers know that many email clients will not support the playback of media content within the email client, so we typically link to our media content from the email and access it in a web browser. But signs are pointing to that not being the case long term, and in some clients its possible to include audio/video playback now.

The Apple Mail email client (version 6.5 and above) supports the <audio> and <video> declarations, as do the iPhone and iPad email clients. In most other email clients, if the audio or video is not supported it will fall back to other content. So you can include audio and video and have a backup that will display if the media content is not supported. But if you know your recipients are on Apple Mail or Apple mobile devices, you can safely include media content.

Visualization

Consumers enjoy visual content. Applications like Pinterest, Instagram, Snapchat, and Vine have shown that images or videos can provide more significant impact than any text message.
Due to the decline in email software use that defaults to images turned off, marketers are now able to rely more on visual content in their messages. As long as the content doesn't require too much bandwidth, everyone should be able to enjoy rich, graphic email on any platform or device.

Some brands are already producing emails that are nearly entirely visual and are reminiscent of visual platforms. This email from Constant Contact shows a Pinterest-style layout.

PART SIX: The Future Of B2B Email Marketing

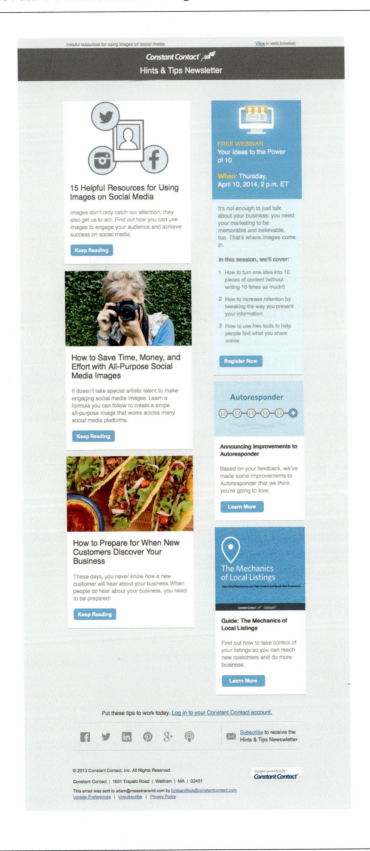

End Notes

1. Jessica E. Vascellaro, "Why Email No Longer Rules...," *The Wall Street Journal*, updated October 12, 2009, accessed December 2, 2013, http://online.wsj.com/news/articles/SB10001424052970203803904574431151489408372.

2. Michael Chui, James Manyika, Jacques Bughin, Richard Dobbs, Charles Roxburgh, Hugo Sarrazin, Geoffrey Sands and Magdalena Westergren, *The Social Economy: Unlocking Value and Productivity Through Social Technologies* (New York: McKinsey Global Institute, 2012), accessed June 4, 2014, http://www.mckinsey.com/insights/high_tech_telecoms_internet/the_social_economy.

3. Chui et al, *The Social Economy*, mckinsey.com

4. "Attention Span Statistics," StatisticBrain, research date January 1, 2014, accessed June 2, 2014, http://www.statisticbrain.com/attention-span-statistics.

5. "Brands' Email Volume Rises Yet Again in Q4 '13; Coupon Messages Outperform Other Promotions," MarketingCharts, published March 3, 2014, accessed June 17, 2014, http://www.marketingcharts.com/online/brands-email-volume-rises-yet-again-in-q4-13-coupon-messages-outperform-other-promotions-41070/.

6. Chui et al, *The Social Economy*, mckinsey.com.

7. "Excerpt: MarketingSherpa Email Marketing Benchmark Survey," MarketingSherpa, published 2013, accessed June 3, 2014, https://www.marketingsherpa.com/data/public/reports/benchmark-reports/EXCERPT-BMR-2013-Email-Marketing.pdf.

8. "How to Measure Digital-Marketing ROI for 2014 and Beyond," FulcrumTech.net, originally published in *NewsLever*™ January 2014, accessed November 22, 2014, http://www.fulcrumtech.net/resources/measure-digital-marketing-roi/.

9. "2012 Channel Preferences Survey," ExactTarget, accessed June 2, 2014, http://pages.exacttarget.com/SFF14-US.

10. Mathew Sweezey, "65% of B2B Buyers Concur Emails Shape Their View of a Company's Brand," ClickZ, published September 26, 2013, accessed October 17, 2014, http://www.clickz.com/clickz/column/2295573/65-of-b2b-buyers-concur-emails-shape-their-view-of-a-company-s-brand.

11. Andrew Dalglish, "Email marketing: Overcoming message overload," Circle Research, published March 26, 2012, accessed December 28, 2013, http://www.circle-research.com/2012/b2b-marcomms/b2b-email-marketing-statistics/.

ENDNOTES

12. "B2B Marketers Point to Email As Their Most Important Digital Tool," MarketingCharts, published March 16, 2013, accessed September 3, 2014, http://www.marketingcharts.com/wp/online/b2b-marketers-point-to-email-as-their-most-important-digital-tool-27555/.

13. Marketing Charts, "B2B Marketers Point to Email As Their Most Important Digital Tool," Marketing Charts, accessed September 3, 2014, http://www.marketingcharts.com/online/b2b-marketers-point-to-email-as-their-most-important-digital-tool-27555/.

14. Graham Charlton, "Email remains the best digital channel for ROI," Econsultancy blog, published March 31, 2014, accessed September 3, 2014, https://econsultancy.com/blog/64614-email-remains-the-best-digital-channel-for-roi.

15. Charlton, "Email remains the best digital channel for ROI," Econsultancy.com.

16. Charlton, "Email remains the best digital channel for ROI," Econsultancy.com.

17. "10 Best Email Practices" Infographic, Madison Logic, published April 9, 2014, accessed June 4, 2014, http://www.madisonlogic.com/10-email-best-practices/.

18. Ayaz Nanji, "Marketing Email Benchmarks: Open Rates, CTRs, Device Trends," MarketingProfs, published June 3, 2014, accessed July 27, 2014, http://www.marketingprofs.com/charts/2014/25246/marketing-email-benchmarks-open-rates-by-industry-device-trends.

19. "The Q4 2013 E-mail Trends and Benchmarks Report," Epsilon, published April 2014, accessed August 2, 2014, http://knowledge.emailinstitute.com/Q42014EmailTrendsBenchmarkReport.

20. Dalglish, "Email marketing: Overcoming message overload," Circle-Research.com.

21. "B2B Email Marketing Best-Practices and Trends," MarketingProfs, published July 25, 2012, accessed June 3, 2014, http://www.marketingprofs.com/charts/2012/8524/b2b-email-marketing-best-practices-and-trends.

22. "B2B Email Marketing Best-Practices and Trends," MarketingProfs.com.

23. Dalglish, "Email marketing: Overcoming message overload," Circle-Research.com.

24. "B2B Email Marketing Best-Practices and Trends," MarketingProfs.com.

ENDNOTES

25. "Excerpt: 2013 Email Marketing Benchmark Report," MarketingSherpa, published March 26, 2013, accessed March 14, 2014, http://www.marketingsherpa.com/article/excerpt/free-excerpt-email-marketing-benchmark-2013.

26. "Excerpt: 2013 Email Marketing Benchmark Report," MarketingSherpa.com.

27. "Research: The Email Subscriber Experience 2008-2013," Return Path, published 2013, accessed March 28, 2014, http://landing.returnpath.com/email-subscriber-experience.

28. Ayaz Nanji, "Email Design and Platform Trends," MarketingProfs, published March 12, 2014, accessed September 1, 2014, http://www.marketingprofs.com/charts/2014/24711/email-design-data-and-platform-trends.

29. "Research: The Email Subscriber Experience 2008-2013," ReturnPath.com.

30. "Free Executive Summary: 2011 B2B Marketing Benchmark Report," MarketingSherpa, published October 27, 2010, accessed September 22, 2013, http://www.marketingsherpa.com/article/2011-b2b-marketing-benchmark-report.

31. "Marketing Research Chart," MarketingSherpa.com.

32. Andrew Dalglish, "It's all about the lead," Circle Research, published June 12, 2012, accessed September 1, 2014, http://www.circle-research.com/2012/its-all-about-the-lead/.

33. "Marketing Research Chart: What is the biggest B2B marketing challenge?," MarketingSherpa, published November 12, 2013, accessed June 3, 2014, http://www.marketingsherpa.com/article/chart/biggest-b2b-marketing-challenge.

34. "More that 40 Percent of Marketers Report that Failing to Innovate with Email Will Result in Loss of Customers", Monetate press release, October 8, 2014, accessed January 22, 2015, http://www.monetate.com/news/more-than-40-percent-of-marketers-report-that-failing-to-innovate-with-email-will-result-in-loss-of-customers/.

35. "1 in 5 Marketers Say They Use Pop-Ups to Collect Email Addresses," MarketingCharts, published January 17, 2013, accessed June 22, 2014, http://www.marketingcharts.com/online/1-in-5-marketers-say-they-use-pop-ups-to-collect-email-addresses-26321/

36. "22% of permissioned email never reaches the inbox," BizReport, published July 31, 2013, accessed August 27, 2014, http://www.bizreport.com/2013/07/22-of-permissioned-email-never-reaches-inbox.html.

ENDNOTES

37. Ayaz Nanji, "How Email Blacklists Affect Marketing Campaigns [Infographic]", MarketingProfs, published June 16, 2014, accessed September 1, 2014, http://www.marketingprofs.com/charts/2014/25363/how-email-blacklists-affect-marketing-campaigns-infographic.

38. Mike Parkinson, "The Power of Visual Communication," Billion Dollar Graphics, modified June 10, 2013, accessed August 8, 2014, http://www.billiondollargraphics.com/infographics.html.

39. Jakob Nielsen, "How Users Read on the Web," Nielsen Norman Group, published October 1, 1997, accessed August 7, 2014, http://www.nngroup.com/articles/how-users-read-on-the-web.

40. "2013 Subject Line Analysis Report," Adestra, published October 24, 2013, accessed March 21, 2014, http://www.adestra.com/resources/downloadable-reports/2013-subject-line-analysis-report/.

41. Dan Zarrella, "Science of Email 2014," Hubspot, published June 25, 2014, accessed June 26, 2014, http://cdn2.hubspot.net/hub/53/file-1100642125-pdf/Science_of_Email_2014_FINAL_AS_OF_JUNE_25-1.pdf.

42. Beth Negus Viveiros, "Enewsletters Outperform B2B Promotional Emails: Study," Chief Marketer, published February 21, 2014, accessed February 27, 2014, http://www.chiefmarketer.com/enewsletters-outperform-b2b-promotional-emails-study.

43. Amy Schade, Janelle Estes, and Jakob Nielsen, "Email Newsletter Usability," Fourth Edition, Nielsen Norman Group, published November 28, 2010, accessed December 29, 2013, http://emarketingadjunct.files.wordpress.com/2011/04/newsletter-usability-4th-edition.pdf.

44. Alex Dalenberg, "Want to reach the top dogs? Executives still love their email newsletters," *Upstart Business Journal*, published May 30, 2014, accessed September 1, 2014, http://upstart.bizjournals.com/companies/media/2014/05/30/want-to-reach-the-top-dogs-executives-still-love.html.

45. Justin Ellis, "Probably not a surprise: Turns out your boss spends a lot of time in email - reading news," NeimanLab, published May 29, 2014, accessed June 14, 2014, http://www.niemanlab.org/2014/05/probably-not-a-surprise-turns-out-your-boss-spends-a-lot-of-time-in-email-reading-news/.

46. David Moth, "Smartphone owners more likely to read emails than make calls: stats," Econsultancy blog, published January 17, 2013, accessed August 7, 2014, https://econsultancy.com/blog/61897-smartphone-owners-more-likely-to-read-emails-than-make-calls-stats.

ENDNOTES

47. Justine Jordan, "53% of Emails Opened on Mobile; Outlook Opens Decrease 33%," Litmus, published January 15, 2015, accessed January 16, 2015, https://litmus.com/blog/53-of-emails-opened-on-mobile-outlook-opens-decrease-33.

48. "Mobile Dependence Day," ExactTarget, modified February 27, 2013, accessed June 23, 2014, http://pages.exacttarget.com/SFF9-US.

49. "Constant Contact and Chadwick Martin Bailey Study: Three-Quarters of Consumers 'Highly Likely' to Delete Emails They Can't Read on Mobile Devices," Constant Contact news release, published August 13, 2013, accessed April 14, 2014, http://news.constantcontact.com/press-release/constant-contact-and-chadwick-martin-bailey-study-three-quarters-consumers-highly-like.

50. "Mobile Dependence Day," ExactTarget.com.

51. "Constant Contact and Chadwick Martin Bailey Study: Three-Quarters of Consumers 'Highly Likely' to Delete Emails They Can't Read on Mobile Devices," Constant Contact news release, published August 13, 2013, accessed April 14, 2014, http://news.constantcontact.com/press-release/constant-contact-and-chadwick-martin-bailey-study-three-quarters-consumers-highly-like.

52. "7 in 10 companies ignore mobile email readership," Adestra, modified October 14, 2013, accessed August 14, 2014, http://www.adestra.com/7-10-companies-ignore-mobile-email-readership.

53. Helen Leggatt, "Study highlights importance of mobile-first email strategies," BizReport, published August 19, 2013, accessed September 21, 2013, http://www.bizreport.com/2013/08/study-highlights-importance-of-mobile-first-email-strategies.html.

54. Adam Q. Holden-Bache, "Mobile Email From Name and Subject Line Displays [Infographic]", Mass Transmit, published July 30, 2013, accessed June 4, 2014, http://masstransmit.com/broadcast_blog/mobile-email-from-name-and-subject-line-displays-infographic.

55. "Email interaction across mobile and desktop," Campaign Monitor, accessed March 11, 2014, http://www.campaignmonitor.com/guides/email-marketing-trends.

56. Helen Leggatt, "Few email marketers using responsive design in all deployments," BizReport, published May 19, 2014, accessed June 4, 2014, http://www.bizreport.com/2014/05/few-email-marketers-using-responsive-design-in-all-deploymen.html.

57. "The 2012 Digital Marketer: Benchmark and Trend Report," Experian, modified April 5, 2012, accessed September 7, 2013, http://go.experian.com/forms/experian-digital-marketer-2012.

ENDNOTES

58. "Video emails improve campaign results. Check out these stats!," GetResponse, published December 8, 2009, accessed June 27, 2013 http://blog.getresponse.com/video-emails-improve-campaign-results-check-out-these-stats.html.

59. "The ROI of Email Relevance: Improving Campaign Results Through Targeting," Jupiter Research, August 2005, quoted in "The Ultimate List of Marketing Statistics," Hubspot.com, last updated April 7, 2014, accessed February 15, 2015, http://www.hubspot.com/marketing-statistics.

60. "Email Marketing: Get Personal with Your Customers," Aberdeen Group, published June, 2008, accessed March 22, 2014, http://www.oldvinemarketing.com/docs/Email-marketing.pdf.

61. Willie Myers, "4 Easy Ways to Personalize Your Emails With Rapleaf," Rapleaf, published August 19, 2013, accessed December 2, 2013, http://www.rapleaf.com/2013/08/19/4-easy-ways-to-personalize-your-emails-with-rapleaf/.

62. Dan Zarella, "Science of Email 2014," Hubspot, accessed June 26, 2014, http://cdn2.hubspot.net/hub/53/file-1100642125-pdf/Science_of_Email_2014_FINAL_AS_OF_JUNE_25-1.pdf.

63. "Personalized Marketing Brings Rewards and Challenges," eMarketer, published June 2, 2011, accessed June 23, 2014, http://www.emarketer.com/Article/Personalized-Marketing-Brings-Rewards-Challenges/1008417.

64. "B2B Email Marketers Focus on Targeting Content," eMarketer, published May 21, 2013, accessed June 24, 2014, http://www.emarketer.com/Article/B2B-Email-Marketers-Focus-on-Targeting-Content/1009908.

65. "B2B Email Marketers Focus on Targeting Content," eMarketer.

66. Jon Miller, "CHART: 23% of Email Engagement Is Explained By Segmentation," Marketo, published August 29, 2013, accessed May 7, 2014, http://blog.marketo.com/blog/2013/08/chart-23-of-email-engagement-is-explained-by-segmentation.html.

67. "CHART: 23% of Email Engagement Is Explained By Segmentation," Marketo.

68. Adam Sutton, "Email Marketing: Big ROI for simple B2B alerts," MarketingSherpa, published April 15, 2014, accessed February 24, 2014, http://www.marketingsherpa.com/article/case-study/email-marketing-b2b-simple-alerts.

69. "B2B Email Marketers Focus on Targeting Content," eMarketer, published May 21, 2013, accessed June 24, 2014, http://www.emarketer.com/Article/B2B-Email-Marketers-Focus-on-Targeting-Content/1009908.

ENDNOTES

70. David Kirkpatrick, "Email Marketing: The importance of lead nurturing in the complex B2B sale," MarketingSherpa, published January 19, 2012, accessed June 24, 2014, http://sherpablog.marketingsherpa.com/email-marketing/b2b-lead-nurturing-importance/.

71. "B2B's Digital Evolution," Google, published February 2013, http://www.google.com/think/articles/b2b-digital-evolution.html.

72. "MarketingSherpa 2011 B2B Marketing Benchmark Report," MarketingSherpa, published October 27, 2010, accessed September 22, 2013, http://www.marketingsherpa.com/article/2011-b2b-marketing-benchmark-report.

73. "Top Reasons for Unsubscribing From an Email Program," Marketing Charts, accessed March 4, 2014, http://www.marketingcharts.com/wp/topics/email/one-more-time-email-frequency-chief-culprit-in-unsubscribes-27944/attachment/bluehornet-email-unsubscribe-reasons-mar2013.

74. "2014 Marketing Automation Trends Unveiled for B2B Marketers by Regalix," IT Business Net, published May 15, 2014, accessed December 12, 2014, http://www.itbusinessnet.com/article/2014-Marketing-Automation-Trends-Unveiled-for-B2B-Marketers-by-Regalix-3258807.

75. "Marketing Research Chart: Most popular email elements to test," MarketingSherpa, published September 25, 2012, accessed March 4, 2014, http://www.marketingsherpa.com/article/chart/top-email-elements-to-test.

76. Ginger Conlon, "Which ESPs Give Email Marketers ESP?" Direct Marketing News, accessed February 27, 2015, http://www.dmnews.com/which-esps-give-email-marketers-esp/article/399704/.

77. "The S.A.M.E. (Support Adoption of Metrics for Email) Project," Direct Marketing Association, accessed September 21, 2013, https://emailexperience.org/email-resources/email-research-and-projects/support-adoption-of-metrics-for-email-project/.

78. "Marketing Research Chart: Email marketing ROI," MarketingSherpa, published March 5, 2013, accessed February 23, 2014, http://www.marketingsherpa.com/article/chart/email-marketing-roi-marketers-perceptions.

79. "The Power of Direct Marketing: ROI, Sales, Expenditures and Employment in the US, 2011-2012 Edition," DMA, published October 2011, accessed January 4, 2014, http://imis.the-dma.org/bookstore.

80. "B2B Email Marketing Best-Practices and Trends," MarketingProfs, published July 25, 2012, accessed March 30, 2014, http://www.marketingprofs.com/charts/2012/8524/b2b-email-marketing-best-practices-and-trends.

81. "2015 Marketing Trends Survey," StrongView, accessed December 28, 2014, http://media.strongview.com/pdf/StrongView_2015_Marketing_Trends_Results.pdf.

82. Bola Awoniyi, "Four innovations that will shape the future of email marketing," Econsultancy, published April 21, 2014, accessed April 21, 2014 https://econsultancy.com/blog/64691-four-innovations-that-will-shape-the-future-of-email-marketing.

83. "Four innovations that will shape the future of email marketing," Econsultancy.

Acknowledgements

Without the support and assistance of a number of people this book would have never come to fruition.

I'd like to start by thanking my wife, Sarah, and my boys, Dylan and Brady, for their support and for putting up with my ridiculousness, which extends well beyond the writing of this book.

I'd also like to thank my mother, Myra Ault, for her life-long support and for providing a foundation for success.

Thanks also goes to my father, Harold Bache. The "4Ds" apply to the written word as well!

Shout outs to my brothers, Chad and Hal Holden-Bache, and my sister, Julie Jones, as well as their families. I've been privileged to have an awesome family, and their support means a lot to me. Same holds true for my aunt, Patricia Devescovi, and all my other immediate and extended family.

I have to say thanks to all my former co-workers at Mass Transmit, as they were working right along with me for the thousands of email campaigns we prepared and delivered over the past 18+ years. Special thanks to my business partners Mark Lewis and Anthony Schneider, and long term employees Marla Chupack, Christian Skelly, Jamie Allen, and Rich Barrett. And cheers to my new family at Striata Inc. I look forward to being a part of many more campaigns to come!

It's entirely likely this book would have never seen the light of day if it weren't for writer/author/adventurer Tamela Rich. Her writing masterclass provided the initial inspiration, and her assistance framing the theme and content for the book played a huge role in getting the book started and completed. She also provided motivation and lots of great advice, and for that I owe her a huge thank you.

I'd have also been lost without the assistance of SPARK Publications. Fabi Preslar and her team provided everything I required to get the book from digital file to finished product. Huge thanks to Melisa K. L. Graham for her editing and management skills, to Larry Preslar for the book layout and cover design, and to everyone else at SPARK who contributed to the design, production, and marketing of this book.

All charts in this book are the creative talent of former Mass Transmit graphic designer Jamie Allen. His skill was instrumental in providing the initial creative direction, color schemes, and more. He is also

ACKNOWLEDGEMENTS

responsible for the development of the http://b2bemailmarketingbook.com web site. You can see more of his work at http://jamieallen.co.

I'd like to extend a special thanks to Scott Hardigree and Anthony Schneider for providing proof reading and feedback on my initial drafts.

Thanks also to Jeffrey L. Cohen at B2BSocialMedia.com for allowing me to publish B2B marketing blog posts on his site. Some of those posts were my first real exposure to a large audience, which gave me confidence to continue onto bigger projects.

Being a member of the email marketing group Only Influencers has also been extremely beneficial. The discussion around the most relevant and timely email marketing topics has certainly improved my email marketing knowledge. I've learned a lot from the likes of Dela Quist, Loren McDonald, Justine Jordan, Jordie van Rijn, Karen Talevera, Jordan Cohen, and many others. And special thanks to Bill McCloskely for managing the OI group.

The Business Marketing Association (BMA) has been my lifeline to the B2B marketing community. From serving on the board at the BMA Carolinas to being involved in national-level activities and conferences, I've been exposed to some of the brightest B2B minds and top-level B2B content and participated in fantastic B2B events. I urge any B2B marketer to get involved with their regional chapter. Learn more at http://marketing.org.

Also, I'd like to thank everyone who assisted in helping me assemble the case studies. I originally had over 12 case studies to include, but due to various reasons many were unable to be published. For those that are included, I thank Lindsey Wagner from Fierce Markets, Scott Hardigree from Indiemark, Jeroen Ederveen of Exact Software, Marty Metro from UsedCardboardBoxes.com, and Sherry Lamoreaux from Act-On Software for their help and assistance with the case study content and approvals.

Lastly, I'd like to thank all the B2B marketers out there. You were the inspiration for the book, and I sincerely hope it has provided some level of insight or value to your email marketing efforts. I wish you continued success.

— Adam

PS—If you've made it this far, please feel free to reach out to me with any feedback/comments at adam@b2bemailmarketingbook.com, and please connect with me on LinkedIn. I would also deeply appreciate any reader reviews on the sites where this book may be purchased. Thank you!

Your Notes

YOUR NOTES

YOUR NOTES

YOUR NOTES

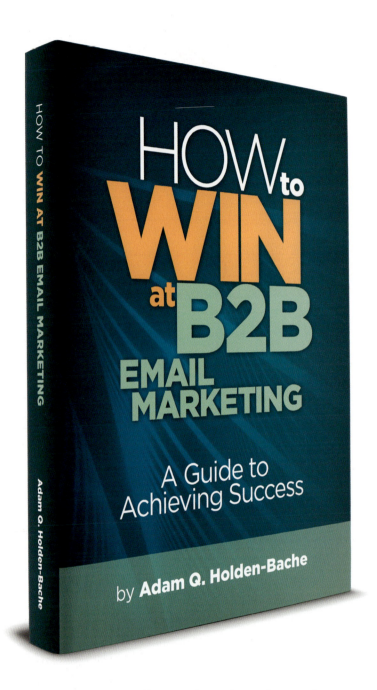

www.b2bemailmarketingbook.com